The " Teaching of English" Series

General Editor—SIR HENRY NEWBOLT

EARLIER ENGLISH DRAMA

No. 55

The Maypole at St. Andrew Undershaft.

(Showing the May-Day sports. See page 18.)

EARLIER ENGLISH DRAMA

FROM ROBIN HOOD TO EVERYMAN

Edited and Arranged for Acting
by
F. J. TICKNER, B.A. (Oxon.)

THOMAS NELSON & SONS, Ltd.
LONDON AND EDINBURGH

First published July 1926

PRINTED IN GREAT BRITAIN AT
THE PRESS OF THE PUBLISHERS

CONTENTS

v

INTRODUCTION

FIFTY years ago the plays performed in England during the Middle Ages were known only to a small number of scholars. Nowadays they are becoming more and more a matter of general interest, and one object of the present book is to make it possible for some of them to be read by those who have no specialized knowledge of the English in which mediæval drama was produced.

The number of plays which have survived in written form is relatively large; and so selection has been necessary. In making this selection two things had to be remembered. In the first place, the same stories are often found in plays which were performed in different parts of the country. And secondly, these plays are not always at the same stage of development. Therefore, whilst this book attempts to include a variety of the subjects which were presented on the stage in the Middle Ages, one story, that of Noah's flood, has deliberately been repeated in three different versions to show how much cruder the earlier plays were. There are also two versions of the story of the Nativity, both admirably suited for simple dramatic representation.

It has of course been necessary to modernize the spelling and some of the words of the original. Every effort has been made to retain the mediæval spirit of the plays, but omissions have had to be made where lines were unsuitable or uninteresting. These changes have occasionally been made at the expense of the rime; sometimes also the rime has been lost merely through alterations in pronunciation since the Middle Ages.

These plays were written for simple-minded people, and so to us they may seem clumsy and slow. Moreover, the modern world has lost that intense religious belief and feeling which the mediæval audience possessed. But this very simplicity makes the plays admirably suited for amateur performances, especially for performances by children and young people. The subject-matter is well known, there are no complicated situations to unfold, and there are enough humorous passages to give scope for comic as well as for serious actors. Simple representations in school and elsewhere will do much more for an understanding of the plays than mere reading ever can. To help in such representations notes and illustrations have been added, and it is hoped that these will prove serviceable, although they make no pretence of suggesting the only way in which the plays can be produced.

A short bibliography has been added for the benefit of those who wish to pursue their studies further in this interesting branch of the English drama.

NOTES ON THE STAGING OF THESE PLAYS

The Stage

A picture of a mystery play in progress is to be found on page 148, but it must be remembered that for a modern production a movable stage, a " pageant " as it was called, is not suitable. We can assume, then, that an ordinary rectangular stage is to be used for our representation of a mediæval play.

The first problem is of course the scenery. Scenes, as we know them, are an invention of the sixteenth and seventeenth centuries, so that for one of these plays there is no need of elaborate painted settings. The great objective in this case is simplicity, and the best effects will probably be obtained from plain curtains. The colour of the curtains might be suggestive of the scene which is taking place : for a daytime scene light-coloured curtains should be used, for a night scene, dark ones. A change of scene could be effected by altering the curtain at the back of the stage.

It is perhaps difficult to present heaven on a modern stage. In the Middle Ages it was customary for an actor, representing God, to sit in glory on a platform at the back. In a modern production it would be both more reverent and more effective to do away with this altogether, and merely to let the voice of God be heard, speaking from above. On the other hand, there is no reason why angels should not appear in the clouds. This can easily be done by putting them on a raised platform at the back of the stage, in front of which can be draped blue and white curtains to represent the sky. Where electric light is possible, it would be effective to light up heaven more brightly than the earth below.

Besides heaven there is also hell, and although hell was imagined to be below the earth, the players of the Middle Ages were usually content to represent only the mouth of hell on the stage itself. What this was like can easily be seen from the illustration on page 127. For a modern production hell mouth can easily be constructed with cardboard or cloth on a wooden frame. It can be made more realistic by concealing in it a red electric bulb to represent the glow of the eternal fire ; and further decorations can be added in the way of imitation flames, made by fastening red and yellow ribbons on to an electric fan. A modern producer might wish to conceal the mouth of hell during scenes in which the devil does not have to enter. In mediæval times it seems to have been a permanent feature at one side of the stage, ready for the devil whenever he wanted to use it. But this is a matter for the individual taste of the producer.

The Characters

Before considering the particular characters of
each play, it is as well to form a general idea of
the kind of effect which is most to be desired.   Evidence is fairly conclusive that in the fifteenth century
the costume of people on the stage was much the same
as the costume of people off the stage.   In a modern
production this rule is impossible, since to our eyes
Bible characters would look ridiculous in modern dress.
We are left, therefore, with two alternatives.   The
costumes may represent as nearly as possible the costumes which may have been in use at the time when
the action is supposed to take place, or they may represent the costumes of the fifteenth century.   Of these
alternatives the second is probably the more satis-
factory, for, as we shall see, the plays were to a large
extent "modernized" by the fifteenth-century players.
Representations of fifteenth-century men and women,
and devils and angels, may be taken from contemporary pictures or stained glass, from which sources most
of the illustrations of this book have been obtained.
For a play on such a well-known theme as the Nativity, it would also be possible to take paintings by
some particular school of artists, Italian or Flemish
or Dutch, and to copy the costumes from them.

In costume, as in staging, the great objective is
simplicity.   Each character should have some typical
object which marks him out at once.   A king should
wear his crown, a bishop his mitre, a woman her
cloak.   A knight would carry sword and lance, a
shepherd his crook and horn.   An angel should be
dressed in white and gold with wings on his back, just
as a devil should be dressed in black with a tail, and
possibly with horns on his head.

Notes on Individual Plays

The Robin Hood Play.—This is a very simple play to stage. The scene is Sherwood Forest, so that it would make a very good play for open-air acting. Robin Hood and his men should be clad in suits of Lincoln green, after the manner of the illustration on page 21, and the potter and his boy should be in similar costume, but not in clothes of a green colour. Robin should have a sword ; his men should have staves, and bows and arrows. Any one who wishes to elaborate this little play can easily do so from the *Ballad of Robin Hood and the Potter*.

Noah's Flood.—The main difficulties of this play are the flood and the ark. The flood must be left to the imagination acting upon the information given in the text, but where electric lighting is possible it would be effective to darken the stage when the rain starts, and to make it brighter when the floods are stayed. Lightning can easily be made by electricity, and a common method of imitating thunder is to rattle a sheet of tin or other metal. The ark would no doubt take the form of an enlarged version of the ark so familiar in toy-shops. It could be prepared in four or five pieces, so that Noah and his sons could carry it on to the stage and build it up at the back. The animals would have to be representative, and no doubt would be enlarged cardboard versions of the usual " Noah's ark " animals. An enterprising producer might also devise a cardboard or paper dove and raven. Noah is suggested by the picture on page 61, and his sons would be dressed in much the same way but without beards. The women's dresses can be copied from one of the pictures of women. The voluminous skirts of the fifteenth century are quite unsuitable for going on board ship, but this would add amusement to the scene. In the Wakefield play Noah's wife must have a distaff and some wool to spin.

The Creation.—The actual scene of the Creation is almost impossible for acting purposes. For the benefit of any one who wishes to attempt the Fall of Lucifer, we offer the information that in the mediæval play Lucifer was represented as an archangel with wings, but on his expulsion from heaven his feathers became torn, and his clothes blackened.

The Prophets.—The prophets would only make a sort of prologue to one of the New Testament plays, whose events they foretell. Prophets would be dignified old men like the one depicted on page 83.

The Nativity and the Massacre of the Innocents.—In these plays it is essential to have a curtain which can be let down to cover the back of the stage. A great deal of the acting can take place in front of this curtain, which must be raised to show the following scenes: (1) The manger at Bethlehem, represented in some simple fashion ; (2) the scene in heaven when the angels sing to the shepherds ; (3) the palace of Herod, which should have a large chair for Herod's throne, and a table on which his banquet may be spread. The star which appears to the shepherds can be represented simply by an electric bulb. But in a more pretentious production, a spot-light in the wings (an ordinary projector lantern) can be used. The star itself will thus not be seen, but its beams will shine across the stage in contrast to a dark background, and in the manger scene can be directed on to Mary and her Child. The kings may come on to the stage from among the audience—a mediæval tradition which may be found effective also in other plays. Several of the characters are suggested by illustrations—Mary (page 116), Joseph (page 87), one of the kings (page 95), a knight (page 121), a shepherd (page 109), and an angel (page 72). In accordance with long-established tradition, Mary should wear a blue dress. Herod was usually represented as a Saracen warrior, and there was a tradition that he should wear a helmet and a blue gown : but he can be depicted as almost any kind of pompous ruler. In accordance with tradition the third king should be a negro, but this is not essential. The armour may seem difficult for a simple production, but so long as the knight has a lance and some sort of a helmet, a white surcoat with a design or a coat of arms on the breast covers up a good deal. A sword and shield add to the effect, and chain armour can be imitated by knitting with thick string and painting over with aluminium paint.

The Raising of Lazarus.—Here again the drop curtain will be useful, for behind it can be prepared the tomb of Lazarus, to which Jesus and the disciples came. The tomb should be a cave or sepulchre, and Lazarus can be laid out on a shelf within it. The characters are quite ordinary people, and should all wear simple dresses. The grave-clothes for Lazarus can be made from a sheet, with a separate piece of white stuff for the sudary, or cloth for the head.

The Betrayal.—The inside of the house can be represented by a table and seats at the back of the stage, so that the drop curtain can be let down in front for the outdoor scenes. A cup for the wine, a dish for the bread, and a bowl for the washing of the disciples' feet are required, as well as a sword for Malchus. Here again all the characters are simple folk, and the priests' servants should be as ruffian-like a crowd as possible. Judas, by tradition, should have a red beard, and Peter a white one.

The Trial.—Here the curtain will have to be raised to show the judgment halls of Pilate and of Herod. The essential thing about a judgment hall is the seat of justice for the governor. In this play a change of judgment seat would be enough to mark the change of place, but other simple alterations of obvious features add to the effect. A knowledge of Scripture supplies the information that Peter must be warming his hands when he betrays our Lord : no doubt other things of this kind may be suggested by a reading of the Bible accounts. Pilate was represented as the governor of a mediæval city, and the Coventry Pilate can be seen on page 148, together with Annas and Caiaphas, who, as we shall have occasion to remark elsewhere, appear as Christian bishops, with mitre and crozier (see also page 198). The doctors and counsellors who give their advice should be dignified men in black, with black gowns (ordinary university gowns would do admirably). Herod would be similar to the Herod of the Nativity play, but not nearly such a blackguard.

The Crucifixion.—This play is almost impossible for simple amateur production, although it is enacted in the Passion play which takes place to this day at Ober-Ammergau in Bavaria.

The Descent into Hell, and the Harrowing of Hell.— For these plays the most essential feature is a pair of large doors for the gates of hell. In the "harrowing" the scene should take place in a red light, for hell fire, and it would also be effective to represent heaven above. Sathanas and his principal subordinates could be represented as fallen angels with torn and dirty wings ; but the ordinary devils should be of the kind shown on page 127.

The Resurrection.—This should be staged in much the same way as *The Raising of Lazarus*, with additional characters who have been discussed in connection with the Trial scene.

The Conversion of Paul.—This play presents few difficulties except the horse which Saul rides to Damascus. This had best be left out, as stage horses are rarely effective. Saul should be represented as a bold warrior, Ananias as a kindly old man, Annas and Caiaphas, as in the trial scene, as bishops (see page 198).

The Morality and *Everyman.*—The scenery for a morality should be vague, since the place where such characters meet one another is almost impossible to imagine. The *Morality of Wisdom* gives some good stage directions, which show how the characters should be dressed, and for *Everyman* much the same thing is required. *Everyman*, himself, should be quite an ordinary person, as suggested on page 230. An abstract figure like Good Deeds or Five Wits can only be depicted as a woman in white, but with some characters more definite costume is possible. Strength should be a strong man, Fellowship a jolly boon-companion, Confession an old father-confessor, Beauty a beautiful person, and so on. Death can either be a dark figure in a sinister cloak, or a gaunt figure with a skeleton painted on his clothes. He may also carry a spear or a drum. A Vice was to be recognized by his wooden sword. Shakespeare in *Twelfth Night* speaks of "the old vice . . . with dagger of lath."

NOTES ON BOOKS FOR FURTHER STUDY

The best work on the subject as a whole is Chambers on *The Mediæval Stage*. A more concise account is to be found in Professor Henry Morley's *First Sketch of English Literature*.

May Day.—The account of the Londoners' Maying is from Stow's *Survey of London*, made in 1603, of which many editions exist. This work contains also the full account of the Mumming in honour of Prince Richard in Chapter III. The May Day Song is from *British Popular Customs*, by T. F. Dyer, 1876. The Robin Hood play is from the fifth volume of Child's *English and Scottish Popular Ballads* (Houghton, Mifflin), where other plays and ballads of Robin Hood are to be found.

Christmas.—The account of the Sword Dance is from the *Gentleman's Magazine* of 1811, and the Sword Dancers' interlude from Bell's *English Poets*, published in 1857. For the Christmas play itself the best sources are an old book by Sandys, entitled *Christmastide*, and the more recent publications of the Folk-lore Society.

Royal Entries.—For the full account of Henry the Fifth's entry the best authority is Sir Harry Nicholas's *History of Agincourt*, from which the account in this book is selected.

The Cornish Plays.—The best edition of Keigwin's translation is that of Davies Gilbert, published in 1827.

The Newcastle Shipwrights' Play is given in full in T. Sharp's *Dissertation on the Ancient Mysteries of Coventry*, 1825. A better edition is in *Non-cycle Mystery Plays*, by the Early English Text Society.

The Wakefield Plays.—Editions of the Towneley plays have been published by the Early English Text Society and by the Surtees Society (1836).

The Play of Coventry, or Ludus Coventriae, also called *The Plaie of Corpus Christi*, was edited by J. O. Halliwell for the Shakespeare Society in 1841. There is also a recent edition by the Early English Text Society.

The Pageant of Shearmen and Taylors.—An edition was published by T. Sharp in 1817, and the play has since been published by the Early English Text Society.

The Chester Plays.—Besides the edition of the Early English Text Society there is an earlier one by T. Wright for the Shakespeare Society, 1843.

The Conversion of Saint Paul and the Morality of Wisdom are from the *Ancient Mysteries from the Digby Manuscripts*, published by the Abbotsford Club (Edinburgh) in 1835, and subsequently by the Early English Text Society.

Everyman.—The first printed edition, on which this copy is based, is that of John Scot about 1520. This book is very rare, but modern editions are numerous ; as many as ten have already appeared in the present century.

For further information about contemporary dress probably the two most useful works are N. H. J. Westlake's *History of Design in Painted Glass*, and A. Parmentier's *Album Historique*.

EARLIER ENGLISH DRAMA

CHAPTER I.—MAY DAY

> Remember, remember
> The fifth of November,
>   Gunpowder treason and plot.
> I see no reason
> Why gunpowder treason
>   Should ever be forgot.

EVERYBODY in England must have heard of Guy Fawkes' Day, when fireworks are let off and the " guy " is burned in the midst of a huge bonfire. During the day itself boys carry round in the streets the " guys " which they have made of straw and old clothes, ready for burning in the evening ; and all day long they ask passers-by to " Spare a penny for the poor old guy."

Now this custom can be traced back to the attempt of a band of conspirators to blow up King James I. and his Parliament on November the fifth, 1605. Guy Fawkes was the man chosen to light the fuse which would fire the charge of gunpowder. Ever since the failure of this plot, the " Fifth " has been celebrated with bonfires and fireworks. But while Guy Fawkes' Day goes back only to the year 1605, there are other days of public rejoicing which go back so far that their origins are completely lost in the mists of antiquity. And one of the most important of these is May Day.

It was the custom in Old England, and in many places it is the custom still, for May Day to be celebrated with great festivity. But in few places nowadays is there anything like the ceremony which took place in London in the time of Queen Elizabeth, when " the citizens of all estates, generally in every parish, and in some instances two or three parishes joining together, had their several Mayings, and did fetch their Maypoles with divers warlike shows ; with good archers, morris-dancers, and other devices for pastime, all day long ; and towards evening they had stage plays and bonfires in the streets. These great Mayings and May games were made by the governors and masters of the city, together with the triumphant setting up of the great shaft or principal Maypole in Cornhill before the parish church of Saint Andrew," which is called St. Andrew Undershaft to this day. A girl was chosen to be " Queen of the May," and to preside over the ceremonies, and sometimes a man or boy was made " Lord of the May " to assist her in this task. But the centre of all their festivities was the Maypole, an upright shaft decorated with flowers, around which dances were performed. Sometimes it was fetched from the woods on the night before, but more usually the pole remained in its place all the year round, and early on May morning bands of young country folk would go out to collect the " May," the hawthorn blossom, with which the Maypole, and the villagers' houses as well, would be decorated. As they came back with their burden they would sing a song, which was always used on this one occasion, just as " Remember, remember," is only used on November the fifth. When this song first began no one can say. Nor are its words exactly the same in every part of England. But in Hertfordshire at the beginning of the last century it was still being sung, and a writer of the period has preserved it for us.

Remember us poor Mayers all,
    And thus we do begin,
To lead our lives in righteousness,
    Or else we die in sin.

We have been rambling all this night,
    And almost all this day,
And now returnèd back again
    We have brought you a bunch of May.

A branch of May we have brought you,
    And at your door it stands,
It is but a sprout, but it's well budded out
    By the work of our Lord's hands.

The hedges and trees they are so green,
    As green as any leek,
Our Heavenly Father, he watered them
    With his heavenly dew so sweet.

The heavenly gates are open wide,
    Our paths are beaten plain,
And if a man be not too far gone
    He may return again.

The life of man is but a span,
    It flourishes like a flower ;
We are here to-day, and gone to-morrow,
    And are dead in an hour.

The moon shines bright, and the stars give light
    A little before it is day.
So God bless you all, both great and small,
    And send you a joyful May.

John Stow mentioned in his account of the Londoners' Maying that they performed stage plays as part of the festivities. The custom of having a play seems to have grown up somewhere about the begin-

ning of the fifteenth century as an addition to the
usual ceremonies of May Day. The hero was the
traditional figure of so many Old English songs,
Robin Hood, the outlaw of Sherwood. Perhaps
before this Robin had become a regular figure at the
May Day feast, and had taken his place alongside the
Queen of the May, with his trusty band of archers in
attendance, all clad in their suits of Lincoln green.
But when Robin Hood appeared, it was very natural
that a few scenes should be played to represent some
of the numerous adventures associated with the great
outlaw. Later on Maid Marian appeared too; but
it seems very likely that she was introduced from
a French story, and so is not of purely English
origin. Only a few fragments of these May Day plays
have been preserved, and of the two which have survived at any respectable length, perhaps this one
of Robin and the Potter makes the better reading.
Even here the story breaks off abruptly at an early
stage in the proceedings.

Enter Robin Hood and his men.

Robin. Listen to me, my merry men all,
And hark what I shall say;
Of an adventure I shall you tell,
That befell the other day.
With a proud potter I met,
And a rose garland on his head,
The flowers of it shone marvellous fresh;
This seven year and more he hath used this way,
Yet was he never so courteous a potter
As one penny passage to pay.
Is there any of my merry men all
That dare be so bold
To make the potter pay passage
Either silver or gold.

    Little John. Not I, master, for twenty pound ready
        told;

For there is not among us all, one
That dares meddle with that potter, man for man.
I felt his hands not long agone,
But I had rather have been here by thee ;
Therefore I know what he is.
Meet him when ye will, or meet him when ye shall,
He is as proper a man as ever you meddled withal.

 Robin. I will lay with thee, Little John, twenty
   pound so red,

A Combat with the Quarter-staff.

(Showing the appropriate dress for Robin Hood and his
men, and for the Potter.)

If I with that potter meet,
I will make him pay passage, at risk of his head.
 Little John. I consent thereto, so eat I bread ;
If he pay passage, at risk of his head,
Twenty pound shall you have of me.

 *Robin and his men hide. The Potter's boy, Jack,
   enters and says :*

Out alas, that ever I saw this day !

For I am clean out of my way
From Nottingham town.
If I hie me not the faster
Ere I come there the market will be done.

   Robin [*as he comes forward*]. Let me see, are the
      pots whole and sound ?
   Jack. Yea, master, but they will not break the
      ground.
   Robin. I will them break, for the rogue thy master's
      sake ;
And if they will break the ground,
Thou shalt have three pence for a pound.

                      [*Robin smashes the pots.*

   Jack. Out, alas ! what have you done ?
If my master come he will break your crown.

The Potter enters, and says to Jack :

Why, thou rascal, art thou here yet ?
Thou shouldst have been at market.

   Jack. I met with Robin Hood, a good yeoman ;
He hath broken my pots
And called you a rogue by your name.

   The Potter [*to Robin*]. Thou mayst be a gentleman,
      so God me save,
But thou seemest a naughty knave.
But if thou be a good fellow,
I will sell my horse, my harness, pots and panniers too ;
Thou shalt have the one half, and I will have the
      other.
If thou be not so content,
Thou shalt have stripes, if thou wert my brother.

   Robin. Hark, Potter, what I shall say ;
This seven year and more thou hast used this way,
Yet wert thou never so courteous to me
As one penny passage to pay.

   Potter. Why should I pay passage to thee ?

   Robin. For I am Robin Hood, chief governor,
Under the greenwood tree.

Potter. This seven year have I used this way up and
down,
Yet paid I passage to no man,
Nor now will I not begin ; so do the worst thou can.
Robin. Passage shalt thou pay here under the
greenwood tree.
Potter. If thou be a good fellow, as men do thee call,
Lay aside thy bow,
And take thy sword and buckler in thy hand
And see what shall befall.
[*They fight, and the Potter uses his quarter-staff with
such goodwill that Robin is forced to call his band.*]
Robin. Little John, where art thou ?
Little John. Here, master, I make God avow.
I told you, master, so God me save,
That you should find the potter a knave.
Hold your buckler fast in your hand,
And I will stiffly by you stand,
Ready for to fight ;
Be the knave never so stout,
I shall rap him on the snout,
And put him to flight.

Unfortunately the rest of the play has been lost,
but we read in the *Ballad of Robin Hood and the
Potter* of how the Potter gave in at this appearance
of superior numbers. The story goes that Robin
borrowed the Potter's wares for the day and dressed
up in the Potter's clothes. Then he went to Nottingham market, and the same poem tells of his adventures there.

CHAPTER II.—CHRISTMASTIDE

BESIDES May Day, Christmas was naturally a time
for jollity and merrymaking of all sorts. But whereas
on May morning the weather is usually fine enough

for the festivities to be held out of doors on the village green, or some such equally suitable spot, at Christmas they must be held for the most part in some fairly large room by the fireside. In the Middle Ages the very natural place for the Christmas merrymaking was in the great hall of the manor-house, whither the villagers would come to share in the good cheer. The merrymaking went on not only at Christmas, but was also carried on over the New Year, usually till Twelfth Night, the sixth of January. This festival was presided over by the " Lord of Misrule," a much less dignified and stately figure than the Queen of the May. The festivities were of a very jovial kind. Heavy eating and sometimes heavy drinking played a prominent part in the Old English Christmas, and even at the present day the custom is far from being forgotten. On the hearth the Yule log blazed merrily, while another feature of the feast was the practice of dressing up in fantastic clothes, a tradition which is still kept up by the paper hats, false noses, and other things to be found in Christmas crackers to this day. Of course the houses were decorated with holly, and the mistletoe bough hung in a prominent position. The morris dancers, too, made their appearance at Christmas time, and they performed a peculiar kind of dance, which in the days of George III. was still being performed on St. Stephen's Night, the twenty-sixth of December, in the north of Yorkshire, where in the year 1811 it was seen by the writer of the following description :

" On the feast of St. Stephen, six youths (called sword dancers, from their dancing with swords), clad in white, and bedecked with ribbons, attended by a fiddler and another youth curiously dressed, who generally has the name of ' Bessy,' and also by one who personates a Doctor, begin to travel from village to village, performing a rude dance, called the sword dance. One of the six acts the part of king in a kind

of farce, which consists of singing and dancing. ' The
Bessy ' interferes while they are making a hexagon
with their swords, and is killed. These frolics they
continue till New Year's Day, when they spend their
gains at the ale-house with the greatest innocence and
mirth, having invited all their rustic acquaintance."

This dance is very interesting, because out of it
grew up what must be one of the oldest plays in the
English language, a play which can be attributed to
no author, since it seems gradually to have come from
the Christmastide dance. It seems fairly certain that
the Robin Hood play was added to the May Day
festival about the beginning of the fifteenth century,
and the Christmastide play is not likely to have been
much older. No doubt it did not begin at the same
time in all parts of the country, and unfortunately no
one seems to have taken the trouble to write it down
till about a hundred years ago. In the description of
the Yorkshire sword dance, we have just seen that a
" kind of farce " was performed. At about the same
time another writer, this time in the county of Dur-
ham, saw a similar dance, which was, however, rather
more like what we should call a play. He describes
it in these words :

*Enter dancers, decorated with swords and ribbons ; the
Captain of the band wearing a cocked hat, and the
Clown, or " Bessy," who acts as treasurer, being
decorated with a hairy cap, and a fox's brush de-
pendent. The Captain forms with his sword a
circle, around which he walks. The Bessy opens
the proceedings by singing :*

Good gentlemen all, to our Captain take heed,
    And hear what he's got for to sing ;
He's lived among music these forty long years
    And drunk of the elegant spring.

Elegant. Probably Bessy means the " Helicon spring."

My mother was burnt for a witch,
    My father was hanged on a tree,
And it's because I'm a fool
    That nobody meddled wi' me.

The dance now commences. It is an ingenious performance, and the swords of the actors are placed in a variety of graceful positions, so as to form stars, hearts, squares, and circles, etc., etc. The dance is so elaborate that it requires frequent rehearsals, a quick eye, and strict adherence to time and tune. Before it concludes, grace and elegance have given place to disorder, and at last all the actors are seen fighting. The Parish Clergyman rushes in to prevent bloodshed, and receives a death-blow. While on the ground, the actors walk round the body, and sing as follows, to a slow psalm-like tune:

Alas! our parson's dead,
    And on the ground is laid;
Some of us will suffer for't,
    Young men, I'm sore afraid.

I'm sure 'twas none of me,
    I'm clear of *that* crime;
'Twas him that follows me
    That drew his sword so fine.

I'm sure it was *not* me,
    I'm clear of that fact;
'Twas him that follows me
    That did this dreadful act.

I'm sure 'twas none of me,
    Who say't be villains all;
For both my eyes were closed
    When our good priest did fall.

A Juggler.
(See page 32.)

The Clergyman. No doubt this does not mean the parson himself, but an actor got up to represent him.

The Bessy sings :

> Cheer up, cheer up, my bonny lads,
> And be of courage brave,
> We'll take him to his church,
> And bury him in the grave.

The Captain speaks. O, for a Doctor,
> A ten pound doctor, oh.

Enter a Doctor, who says :

Here I am, I.

Captain. Doctor, what's your fee ?

Doctor. Ten pounds is my fee !

But nine pounds, nineteen shillings, eleven pence,
three farthings, I will take from thee.

Bessy. There's ge-ne-ro-si-ty !

The Doctor sings :

> I am a doctor, a doctor rare,
> Who travels much at home ;
> My famous pills they cure all ills,
> Past, present, and to come.

> My famous pills, who'd be without,
> They cure the plague, the sickness and gout,
> Anything but a love-sick maid ;
> If *you're* one, my dear, you're beyond my aid.

*Here the Doctor occasionally salutes one of the fair
spectators ; he then takes out his snuff-box, which
is always of very capacious dimensions (a sort of
miniature warming-pan), and empties the contents
(flour or meal) on the Clergyman's face, singing at
the time :*

> Take a little of my nif-naf,
> Put it on your tif-taf ;
> Parson rise and preach again,
> The doctor says you are not slain.

*The Clergyman here sneezes several times, and gradually
recovers, and all shake him by the hand.*

The ceremony terminates by the Captain singing :

> Our play is at an end,
>   And now we'll taste your cheer ;
> We wish you a merry Christmas
>   And a happy New Year.

The Bessy :

> And your pockets full of brass,
> And your cellars full of beer.

> [*A general dance concludes the play.*

In its completest form the Christmas-time play came to represent the story of St. George, the patron saint of England, and it is remarkable how traces appear of its performance in localities all over the country. The healing doctor always comes in, in spite of his complete absence from the usual story of the saint. Readers of the works of Thomas Hardy will remember how the Christmas play is introduced into the story of *The Return of the Native*. In more modern days, when that scene is supposed to have taken place, the villagers went round to give their play in the big farmhouses and other large residences in the neighbourhood, but in the Middle Ages we can imagine the rustic actors coming to perform their play in the hall of some great baron ; just as Shakespeare, who no doubt knew well these country plays, made Peter Quince, Nick Bottom, and the rest of their crew come to play *Pyramus and Thisbe* before the Duke and his court on a slightly different festive occasion, a wedding night.

Here again we are faced with the problem that until the nineteenth century no one took the trouble to put one of these Christmas plays into permanent written form, and by that time a number of alterations had crept into the original story. In Leicestershire, for instance, St. George had been forgotten, and his place taken by Prince George, whose father, the

King of England, represents the Father Christmas of
the West Country version which we have chosen for
our present purpose.

THE CHRISTMAS PLAY OF ST. GEORGE

Enter Father Christmas.

Here come I, old Father Christmas,
    Welcome, or welcome not,
I hope old Father Christmas
    Will never be forgot.

I am not come here for to laugh or to jeer,
But for a pocketful of money and a skinful of beer ;
To show some sport and pastime,
Gentlemen and Ladies in the Christmas-time.
If you will not believe what I do say,
Come in the Turkish Knight—clear the way.

Enter the Turkish Knight.

Open your doors and let me in,
I hope your favours I shall win ;
Whether I rise, or whether I fall,
I'll do my best to please you all.
St. George is here, and swears he will come in,
And if he does, I know he'll pierce my skin.
If you will not believe what I do say,
Come in the King of Egypt—clear the way.

Enter the King of Egypt.

Here I, the King of Egypt, boldly do appear.
St. George, St. George, walk in, my son and heir.
Walk in, my son, St. George, and boldly act thy part,
That all the people here may see thy wondrous art.

Enter St. George.

Here come I, St. George, from Britain did I spring,
I'll fight the Dragon bold, my wonders to begin.

I'll clip his wings, he shall not fly ;
I'll cut him down, or else I die.

Enter the Dragon.

Who's he that seeks the Dragon's blood,
And calls so angry, and so loud ?
That English dog, will he before me stand ?
I'll cut him down with my courageous hand.
With my long teeth, and scurvy jaw,
Of such I'd break up half a score,
And stay my stomach till I'd more.

St. George and the Dragon fight : the latter is killed.

Father Christmas. Is there a doctor to be found
    All ready, near at hand,
To cure a deep and deadly wound,
    And make the champion stand ?

Enter Doctor.

Ah ! yes, there is a doctor to be found,
    All ready, near at hand,
To cure a deep and deadly wound,
    And make the champion stand.
    Father Christmas. What can you cure ?
    Doctor. All sorts of diseases,
Whatever you pleases,
The phthisic, the palsy, and the gout ;
Whatever disorder, I'll soon pull him out.
    Father Christmas. What is your fee ?
    Doctor. Fifteen pounds, it is my fee,
    The money to lay down ;
But as 'tis such a rogue as he,
    I'll cure him for ten pound.
I have a little bottle of Elicumpane,
    Here Jack, take a little of my flip-flop,
    Pour it down thy tip-top,
Rise up and fight again.

The Doctor gives his medicine. The Dragon comes to life again, and fights with St. George, and again is killed.

    St. George. Here I am, St. George, that worthy champion bold,

And with my sword and spear I've won three crowns of gold :

I've found the fiery Dragon, and brought him to the slaughter ;

By that I've won fair Sabra, the King of Egypt's daughter.

    The Turkish Knight advances.

Here come I, the Turkish Knight,
Come from the Turkish land to fight.
I'll fight St. George, who is my foe,
I'll make him yield before I go :
He brags to such a high degree,
He thinks there's none can do the like of he.

    St. George. Where is the Turk that will before me stand ?

I'll cut him down with my courageous hand.

They fight : the Turkish Knight is overcome, and falls on one knee, saying :

Oh ! pardon me, St. George, pardon of thee I crave.
Oh ! pardon me this night, and I will be thy slave.

    St. George. I'll never pardon a Turkish Knight ;

So rise thee up again, and try thy might.

They fight again, when the Knight is killed, and a scene with Father Christmas occurs as before, and the Knight is cured. The Doctor has a basin of girdy grout given him, and a kick, and is driven out. Fair Sabra now comes forward to St. George.

    Father Christmas. Now, ladies and gentlemen, your sport is just ended,

        Girdy grout, Coarse gruel.

So prepare for the box, which is highly commended.
The box it would speak, if it had but a tongue :
Come throw in your money and think it no wrong.

CHAPTER III.—MUMMERS AND GLEEMEN

BESIDES these great feasts of May Day and Christmas,
there was always a demand for amusement in the halls
of the nobility and of the local gentry as well.   From
the oldest times in England it had been the custom for
the noble houses to keep professional story-tellers—
scops, as they were called—who would amuse the guests
after dinner with stories of the great men of old, and
more particularly of the heroic ancestors of the lord of
the house. Besides these there were a large number of
wandering story-tellers—*gleemen*, as the term went—
who roamed up and down the country, now performing in a nobleman's hall, and now singing to rustic folk
on some village green. But the distinction was not
hard and fast ; sometimes a *scop* would go on his
travels seeking better employment, and sometimes a
gleeman would settle down.

But the *gleemen* were only the aristocracy of the
roads in the England of the Middle Ages. From
hall to hall, from village to village, roamed hundreds
of travelling amusement makers. There were the
tumblers, acrobatic dancers, women for the most part,
whose antics included standing on their head and
walking on their hands. It is interesting to find that
in the drawing and sculpture of the time, Salome,
Herodias' daughter, is always depicted standing on
her hands in the attitude of the professional tumbler,
as she may be seen among the carvings at Norwich and
Rouen to this day. Other wanderers of the same class
were tight-rope walkers, jugglers, imitators of animals,
stilt-dancers, and a host of their kind too numerous
to mention. Nor did the tradition die out with the

Middle Ages, for when Queen Mary passed through London to her coronation in 1553, we read that " one Peter, a Dutchman, stood upon the weathercock of Saint Paul's steeple, holding a streamer in his hands of five yards long, and waving thereof. He sometimes stood on one foot, and shook the other, and then he kneeled on his knees, to the great marvel of all the people." For his skill, Peter received sixteen pounds, thirteen shillings and fourpence from the City; but Peter was a master of his craft. The ordinary juggler

Mummers.

and tumbler of the Middle Ages was usually willing to entertain the company for a good dinner and a free night's lodging.

Rather more elaborate than these antics were the mummings, or disguisings, which added to the festivity of the baronial halls. As the name implies, these consisted of dressing up in quaint disguises by bands of roysterers for the amusement of the whole company. The common form of disguising was the imitation of animals, and the wearing of beasts' heads in much the same fashion as Nick Bottom, under rather different circumstances, wore his ass's head in *A Midsummer Night's Dream*. Sometimes the mumming was of the clumsy kind, which provoked Sebastian Brandt to tell how

> " The one hath a visor ugly set on his face,
> Another hath on a vile counterfeit vesture,
> Or painteth his visage with fume in such case,
> That what he is, himself is scantily sure."

But at its best mummery was a very favourite amusement of the nobility. Shakespeare, for example, in *Love's Labour's Lost* makes the King of Navarre and his courtiers dress up as Muscovites for the delectation of the Princess of France. A much earlier mumming was that devised by the citizens of London at the beginning of February 1377, for the amusement of the prince who later in the same year was to become King Richard II., and of his mother, the Princess Joan. It is thus described by the chronicler John Stow :

> " On the Sunday before Candlemas, in the night, one hundred and thirty citizens, disguised, and well horsed, in a mummery, with sound of trumpets, sackbuts, cornets, shawms, and other minstrels, and innumerable torchlights of wax, rode from Newgate, through Cheap, over the Bridge, through Southwark, and so to Kennington, where the young prince remained with his mother, and the Duke of Lancaster, his uncle, with divers other lords. In the first rank did ride forty-eight in the likeness and habit of esquires, two and two together, clothed in red coats and gowns of say or sandal, with comely visors on their faces ; after them came riding forty-eight

---

Brandt, A town clerk of Strassburg and author of a German satire entitled the *Ship of Fools*, which was translated into English by Alexander Barclay and published in 1508.

Fume, Soot.   *Sackbut*, A kind of trumpet.

Shawm, A wind instrument something like a clarinet.

Say, A kind of serge or woollen cloth.   *Sandal*, A light silk stuff.

knights in the same livery of colour and stuff; then followed one rightly arrayed like an emperor; and after him at some distance, one stately attired like the Pope, whom followed twenty-four cardinals, and after them eight or ten with black visors, not amiable, as if they had been legates from some foreign princes. These maskers, after they had entered Kennington, alighted from their horses, and entered the hall on foot; which done, the prince, his mother, and the lords, came out of the chamber into the hall, whom the said mummers did salute, showing by a pair of dice upon the table their desire to play with the prince, which they so handled that the prince did always win when he cast them. Then the mummers set to the prince three jewels, one after another, which were a bowl of gold, a cup of gold, and a ring of gold, which the prince won at three casts. Then they set to the prince's mother, the duke, the earls, and other lords, to every one a ring of gold, which they did also win. After which they were feasted, and the music sounded, the prince and lords danced with the mummers; which jollity being ended, they were again made to drink, and then departed in order as they came."

CHAPTER IV.—ROYAL ENTRIES

BESIDES these occasional mummings, the citizens of London made great festivity on the occasion of royal processions through their city, and of course of their Lord Mayor's Show. Not only was the city gaily decorated, but pageantry of all kinds was introduced, of a much more elaborate kind than that which still takes place on Lord Mayor's Day. Some idea of what these mediæval pageants were like can be gained from the following account of King Henry V.'s victorious home-coming from Agincourt. These selections only tell of a few leading incidents in the elaborate festival.

" At the approach to the Bridge, as it were at the entrance to the authorities of the city, there was erected on the top of the tower a gigantic statue of amazing magnitude, which was looking upon the king's face. He bore, as if a champion, a great axe in his right hand ; but held in his left, as porter, the keys of the city hanging on a staff ; at his right stood a female, not much less in size, clad in a scarlet mantle, as if they were man and wife. Around them banners of the royal arms adorned the tower, elevated in the turrets ; and trumpets, clarions, and horns sounded in various melody. And in front there was this elegant and suitable inscription on the wall : CIVITAS REGIS JUSTICIÆ (The city to the king's righteousness).

" Over the foot of the bridge across the road was raised a tower, in the middle of which stood a most beautiful image of St. George, armed, excepting his head, which was adorned with a laurel wreath. In his right hand he held the hilt of the sword with which he was girded, and in his left a roll, which extended along the turrets, containing the words SOLI DEO HONOR ET GLORIA (To God alone honour and glory).

" And in a contiguous house behind the tower were innumerable boys, representing the angelic host, arrayed in white, and with countenances shining with gold, and glittering wings, and with locks set with precious sprigs of laurel ; who at the king's approach sang with melodious voices and with organs this English anthem :

> " ' Our king went forth to Normandy
> With grace and might of chivalry,
> Our God for him wrought marvellously,
> Wherefore England may call, and cry :
> > Deo gratias,
> Deo gratias, Anglia redde pro victoria,' "

and so on.

Deo gratias, etc. "Glory to God, give glory to God, O England, for thy victory."

" And when they were come as far as the tower of the conduit in Cornhill, the tower was found decked with crimson cloth, spread out after the fashion of a tent upon poles covered with the same cloth. Under the pavilion was a company of prophets, of venerable hoariness, dressed in golden coats and mantles, with their heads covered and wrapped in gold and crimson ; who, when the king passed by them, sent forth a great quantity of sparrows and other small birds, as a sacrifice agreeable to God in return for the victory, and of which some alighted on the king's breast, some rested on his shoulders, and some fluttered round about him : and the prophets sang with sweet harmony a psalm of thanksgiving.

" In the entrance to the street of Cheap were men of venerable old age in apostolic array and number, having the names of the twelve apostles written upon their foreheads, together with the twelve kings, martyrs, and confessors of the succession of England, girded with golden girdles, sceptres in their hands, the express emblems of sanctity, who chanted with one accord at the king's approach a sweet tune.

" When the royal procession proceeded further to the cross of Cheap, the cross was not to be seen ; but as it were, a very fair castle around it, which, constructed with wood with no less ingenuity than excellence, was ornamented with towers and bastions in elegant assemblage. From the middle of the castle, toward the king, a fair portal projected, from which was extended a wooden bridge, covered and decked with tapestry, and reaching the ground. Upon this bridge there proceeded out of the castle to meet the king a chorus of most beautiful girls, elegantly attired in white dresses, singing with timbrel and dance, as to another David coming from the slaughter of Goliath, this song of congratulation : *Welcome Henry the Fifth, King of England and France*. From the top to the bottom of the castle, in the towers, bastions, and columns, were innumerable boys, as it were the archangelic and angelic multitude, decked with celestial gracefulness and singing with one accord to the honour of Almighty God, with sweet melody of voice and with organs, this angelic hymn, *Te Deum laudamus* (We praise thee, O God)," and so on.

CHAPTER V.—THE TROPE

Mark 16: 1-8

ONE of the most dramatic and splendid institutions of the Christian world of the Middle Ages was the Mass, the service of the Church. As time went on its ceremonial tended to become more and more impressive. The churches and cathedrals were built on more and more elaborate lines, and stained windows and rich carvings added to the splendour of the religious ceremonies. The Mass, which led up in elaborate ceremonial to the raising of the Host, the commemoration of the supreme sacrifice of Christ, must have been particularly impressive to the simple mediæval folk. And on the great festivals of the Church further ceremonies were added to remind the people, who could not read the Bible for themselves, of the chief events of the gospel story. At Christmas a model of the crib, the manger in which the Child lay, would be erected in the church—a custom which is being revived in some parishes in England at the present day. At Easter a model of the sepulchre was put up, and a crucifix and part of the consecrated Host would be placed therein from Good Friday to Easter Sunday. Gradually around this grew up special services, *tropes* as they were called, in which certain of the priests, or in the monasteries certain of the monks, would personate the leading characters in the story, something after the fashion of the oratorios of more modern times. But these tropes formed a definite part of the divine service, and the officiating priests wore, not the costumes of the parts as actors would do, but their priestly robes.

Tropes of this kind are said to have been instituted by St. Ethelwold, some hundred years or more before the Norman Conquest, for the Benedictine monks at Winchester. The original instructions were printed in Latin, the language in which all the Church services were celebrated at that time, and the following is a translation of the part relating to the service on Easter Sunday. The cross, representing the body of our Lord, would have been placed in the sepulchre on Good Friday, and on the Sunday morning brought out again in representation of the resurrection.

The Easter Trope

Whilst the lesson is being read, let four brothers vest themselves, and let one of them, clothed in an alb just as though he were engaged in any other office, approach the place of the sepulchre quietly, and there sit silent holding a palm in his hand. While the response is being made, let the three remaining brothers come up, all of them dressed in copes, carrying in their hands thuribles full of incense ; and let them approach upon tiptoe the place of the sepulchre, after the manner of men who are looking for something. These motions are performed in imitation of the angel sitting on the tombstone and the women coming with spices to anoint the body of Jesus. So when he that is sitting sees the three draw near to him, lost, as it were, and looking for something, he shall begin to sing sweetly in a gentle voice, " Whom do ye seek ? " And when he has sung this to the end, these three shall make answer with one voice : " Jesus of Nazareth." He shall reply : " He is not here, he is risen, as he foretold. Go ye and tell that he is risen from the dead." On hearing this command the three shall turn to the choir, saying: "Alleluia, the Lord is risen." When this is said, he who sits at the tomb, as though calling them back again, shall say: "Come ye and see the place where he lay." And as he says this he shall rise and lift up the veil and show them the place empty of the cross, with merely the linen cloths laid, wherein the cross had been wrapped. And when this has been seen, they shall place in this same sepulchre the thuribles which they have been carrying, and take up the linen cloth and spread it out towards the clergy, as if to show that the Lord is risen and no longer wrapped in it. They shall sing this antiphon: "The Lord is arisen from the tomb," and lay the linen cloth on the altar. When the antiphon is done, the prior, rejoicing in the triumph of our king, for that he has vanquished death and is arisen, shall begin the hymn, "We praise Thee, O God!" (*Te Deum laudamus*).

[Translated from a book published in 1625 by R. P. C. Reyer, entitled *De antiquitatibus Ordinis Sancti Benedicti in regno Angliæ* (The Antiquities of the Order of St. Benedict in the kingdom of England).]

CHAPTER VI.—THE CORNISH PLAYS

FROM these tropes, which were, after all, half-dramatic services, it was not very long before men got the idea of representing the stories of Scripture in complete theatrical form. This idea may seem crude at the present day ; but in the days before men could read the Scriptures for themselves, it was one of the best and most natural ways for the priest to bring home to his flock the simple truths of the Bible stories. From the scenes at Christmas and Easter the stories were extended both ways, till by the fourteenth century they began with the Fall of Lucifer, continued with the Creation and the Fall of Man, through the Flood and other leading events of the Old Testament to the

Christmas story, and then went on through the Gospel, with a few extra stories from the lives of the Virgin Mary, Saint Paul, and other leading saints, and ended usually with the End of the World and the Last Judgment. At first these performances took place in the church itself under the direct supervision of the priest ; and we may assume that the original stories were pretty closely followed in the dramatic representation. Very little information has survived about these earliest Scripture plays, or, as they came to be called, " Miracle " plays. A certain amount is known of such performances in some of the German towns— Nürnberg, for example—and there is little reason to doubt that the English plays were on much the same lines. The performances seem usually to have taken place in the nave or body of the church. Very often in the earliest times there was no stage as we know it. It has been suggested that at Axbridge, in Somerset, the play took place on the large rood screen under the tower ; but the truth of this theory has never been fully established, although a play was acted inside this church as late as 1581. More often the actors would perform in a clear space in the middle of their audience. At Freiburg, in South Germany, this custom lingered on even after the play had been transferred from the cathedral to the market-square outside.

But it soon became obvious that the inside of the church was not altogether the best place for these plays, and with fine weather a more suitable site presented itself in the churchyard. At Tours, on the Loire, in the thirteenth century, the steps at the west of the cathedral were used instead. A scaffolding was erected thereon. The level of the top step was taken to represent heaven and paradise, and a few steps down there was a lower stage for the earth. Adam and Eve (for the play seems to have represented the Creation and Fall of Man) were driven from the higher to the lower stage. Below, on the ground level, was an enclosed place, in which cries were heard and chains rattled. Out of it came clouds of smoke and players dressed to represent devils. The earliest recorded instance of an out-of-doors play in England comes from Beverley, in Yorkshire, where in 1220 (five years after King John signed Magna Carta), a play entitled *The Resurrection of our Lord* was performed in the churchyard.

But when the play left the church it fell into the hands of the citizens—for the miracle plays naturally took place in the towns ; they were too elaborate for the country villages, which often had only their Christmastide and May Day plays. The next move, as the citizens got more and more control, was to transfer the play from the churchyard to the market-place, where at Louth in Lincolnshire and at Lucerne in Switzerland the play had its yearly performance. In some towns other obvious sites naturally presented themselves, but usually the centre of the town was the scene of its miracle play.

The plays had to be performed on some great public holiday so that all could take their share, either as performers or as spectators, and the most natural choice was necessarily in the summer, when the daylight lasted longest and the weather was likely to be fine for the performance. The favourite day in England for the miracle plays is Corpus Christi Day, the great Church festival of the Middle Ages, which takes place ten days after Whit-Sunday, and then clergy and laity share alike in the processions. This day was not, however, universal. At Chelmsford Midsummer Day was chosen instead, whilst at Norwich the plays took place at Whitsuntide. At York, somewhere about the year 1428, it was thought that the plays interfered with the religious procession of Corpus Christi, and they were transferred to the day before it. It is impossible to give a date when the plays were completely transferred from clergy to citizens, for this event did not occur at the same time in all places, but perhaps the usual time is about the middle of the fourteenth century.

As soon as the citizens got hold of the play, they seem to have been dissatisfied with the simple Bible stories. New characters appear, most of whom are likely sorts of persons connected with the story, but all of whom are drawn from the everyday life of the period. And, as we shall see, the original characters themselves become modernized to an amazing degree. It is not easy to get an idea of the plays before this development took place, as the copies which have come down to us are usually in their later form. But in Cornwall in the early fifteenth century very simple Scriptural plays were being presented in the old Cornish language ; and from these we can form some impression of what the primitive miracle plays were like. The authors here follow the Bible fairly closely, but Cain is made to come and represent to Noah the foolishness of building this ark ; and Noah's wife comes late, and is only just got aboard in time to avoid the flood. We shall see later on what an important part she came to play in the citizens' plays. This play of *Noah's Flood* was first translated from the original Cornish by John Keigwin in 1693.

Noah's Flood

Noah and his Sons are sitting below. God the Father speaks from above.

Sorrow is with me that I made man
Altogether like to myself.
My right hand though I made him,
When he acted against my commandment
Out of Paradise completely
  By the Angel put I him.
The spirit shall not dwell for ever
In the body of any son of man in the world.

And the reason thereof is,
That he is of soft flesh made.
There is not a man serving me,
Full of truth, surely, at all times,
Save Noah, in all this world,
And his wife and his children likewise.
    My will is thus
To make a deluge over all the world,
So that everything be consumed,
    But certain ones, whom I will save.
    Noah [*below*]. Noah the son of Lamech called am I ;
A great lord in all part remembered
    I am, here in this world.
Substance abundantly I have, and good.
I am bound forever
To worship my good Lord,
    And the Trinity that is on high.
    God [*speaks to Noah*]. Noah, come to me now
And hearken to what I shall say.
    Noah. Ready am I, Lord royal.
Thy will speak to me.
    God. Noah, so full is the world now of hypocrisy,
With sin most truly it is defiled ; I can forbear no more
From bringing death on all people but thee,
And thy wife and thy children, and the goods belong-
        ing to thee.
Therefore make haste, go make a ship of planks
        planed,
And in it many dwellings (rooms they shall be called).
On its side thou shalt hole a door ; this, when thou
        hast made it, shall a port be called.
Beams in it thou shalt place, that it may not fall.
Of every sort and kind, male and female likewise
Thou shalt cause to be put in thy ship within.
Every sort of food in this world that destroyeth
        hunger,
For man and beast as well, in thy ship take care that
        there be.

Noah. Mighty Lord, at thy command I will do. So
   quickly I go.
With mine axe newly sharpened, I will hew every piece
   of timber,
And will plane all the planks, and will set every plank
   sure.

   Shem. I will caulk the planks wondrous fine. There
   shall not any water get in it.
When it is done all over, it will be staunch, I undertake.

   Ham. Here is pitch by me provided and ropes of
   every kind.

*Enter Tubal Cain.   Noah and his sons go on building
      the ark as they talk with him.*

   Cain. A wonder it is to me that thou art so foolish,
   Noah.
Wherefore art thou here to build a ship so worthy,
In the middle of the country, far from the sea ?
I esteem thy skill, however,
To go to such a cost.
All thy labour is not worth a cat.
      A fool thou art.
   Noah. My friend, take thou no wonder ;
Thou shalt weep, and many thousands,
Although now thou fallest into laughter.
In the end, without fraud or guile,
      You shall see a deluge quickly.
Warned I am by God the Father,
To make this very ship
To save me and my children
From this same deluge.
You shall see, within a space,
By floods of the greatest water
      All the world shall be drowned.
   Cain. Ah, old churl, thou bald pate !
How wilt thou have this to be ?
All the waters in this world,

Though they were gathered together,
    Shall not make such an end.
But thou art a fool ;
There is not a man in the country
    Will believe thy report in any wise.
Why, what is the matter,
That God should drown the world ?
  Noah. The matter is this ; so much sin is in the
    world,
And not a jot of amendment, that God the Father is
    angry
With all the people of this world.
And sorrow to him is,
Ever the son of man to have made.
Therefore do you amend ;
In that hour, after a good manner,
If you do repent,
    This same plague shall be made void.
  Cain. Who made thee a preacher
To teach here to us ?
I pray, tell me,
Did he charge this speech to thee
    Alone, without any other man here ?
I know here in the country
Many men, to whom speaks God the Father.
Sir, to some of them
He would disclose
    This great destruction and the flood.
  Noah. Good it is to thee to be wise,
And all the people of this world.
Yet will God never, most truly,
Be found a liar, trust thou me ;
    Therefore be advised.
If you will not, a very great vengeance
Will fall upon you before long.
  Cain. It doth not avail me to reason
With thee, Noah, it seems to me.
I will be gone from hence.   *[Exit Tubal Cain.*

Noah. Now the ship is made
Fair and good to my desire.
Of every kind of beasts
Bring quickly to me by couples,
Cattle, and fowls likewise,
Two and two, female and male.

The sons' wives enter ; and all kinds of animals are brought in. They lead the animals into the ark, and Noah, Ham, Japhet, and the three sons' wives go into it.

Shem [*who stands outside the ark, driving in the animals*]. There is no beast nor worm in the world,
Female and male here,
With me ; to you they are brought.
In the ship there are they.   [*He goes into the ark.*
Ham. Ah ! father, now make ready ;
The flood is almost come.
There are men enough in this world,
Before now wisely did say
        That you were foolish,
When you did make the ship,
Here, just in the middle of the land.
Japhet. A scoff they made of it.
The fear of God's anger was not
        On them then, I know of truth.
Noah. The flood now is come.
All the beasts are gone
Into the ship to their kind,
        As was commanded to me.
Come in, my children,
And your wives as well.
The earth is near covered
By the rain from above. [*Noah's Wife enters, on land.*
        Thou woman, come in, would thou be drowned ?
Noah's Wife. Necessary it is to save what we
        have ;
They cost great store of money,

These same things that are here.

      Sweet Noah, thou dost know this.

                          [She goes into the ark.

   Noah. It is now a great way, very truly,

Since we lost the sight of land.

      Wherefore go forth, raven. *[He sends out a raven.*

Fly away now, and see

Land if thou canst find ;

And the dove very surely

I will send full soon.   *[He sends forth a dove.*

   God the Father [*from above*]. Dead is everything that
      was.

I will command anon

The rain, that it stay now.

   Noah. To God the Father be thanks.

The dove is come,   *[The dove returns.*

And with her a green olive branch.

Come no more will the raven,

      Some carrion has she found.

It is now near a year

Since the beginning of the flood.

   God the Father. Noah, I do command thee,

Go forth out of thy ship immediately,

Thy wife and thy children likewise,

Birds, beasts, and every bullock.

   Noah. Much honour to thee, Lord of heaven,

Thou dost help the weak and the strong.

Let us come out, little and great,

Cattle, birds, and beasts,

      All that were in the ship brought.

   They come out of the ship, and Noah makes
            ready to sacrifice.

Raise an altar I will.

Let us sing

And sacrifice now

With this honour to God.

CHAPTER VII.—THE NEWCASTLE SHIPWRIGHTS' PLAY

SINCE these plays were only performed once a year, they could not be done by professional actors, in the sense that we know them now. Nor does it seem that anything of the kind was thought of. The plays fell into the amateur hands of the skilled workmen of the town ; and since those workmen were formed into gilds or associations for the purposes of their craft, it was very natural that the plays should be organized by the gilds too. Sometimes a special gild was formed for the proper organization of the Corpus Christi festival itself. At Lavenham, in Suffolk, this was the case ; and we can imagine the gildsmen there having their great procession on that feast day to the church, which was specially decorated at the expense of the gild funds. After the service a play was staged, probably in this case in the church itself, and then came more pageantry, and in the evening a great feast, for the Corpus Christi gildsmen well knew the attractiveness of a good banquet. But Lavenham was a small town, and in the larger towns, even if a Corpus Christi gild existed to supervise the feast, the plays were parcelled out among the craft gilds, one gild doing each scene. Just as the fifteenth century was the great age of the gilds, so from this connection it became the great age of the gild plays too. Some scholars have suggested that the other name for the miracle plays ("mystery plays") is derived from this association, for a *mystery* was the name given to a *mastery* or trade. The choice of what scene each gild should produce was often a very appropriate one. At York the Shipwrights performed the *Building of the Ark*, and the Fishers and Mariners *Noah's Flood*. The Goldsmiths were responsible for the *Coming of the*

4

Three Kings. Other choices were less obviously connected, like that of the Fullers to do *Adam and Eve in the Garden*. And naturally a number had just to be filled up. At Coventry, as we shall see, the Shearmen and Taylors played the story of the Nativity and the Slaying of the Children.

After the very simple Cornish play it will now be interesting to see how the Shipwrights of Newcastle-on-Tyne performed the same story. This play is still very crude, and the persons in it are figures without the reality which we shall find in later plays; but still there is <u>an attempt to make them seem like real people</u>, and we shall find Noah's wife has become a much more important individual. The devil also appears, and we see the beginning of his career in the mystery plays in which he becomes a most important and essentially a comic figure.

Noah's Ark; or the Shipwrights' Ancient Play or Dirge

God begins: Free was this world that I have wrought.
No marvel it is if I destroy ;
The folk on earth I made of nought,
Now are they fully my foe.
Vengeance now will I do,
On them that have grieved me ill ;
Great floods shall over them go,
And run over heath and hill.
All mankind dead shall be,
With storms both stiff and steer ;
All but Noah, my darling free,
His children and their wivës dear.
Evermore yet their trust was in me,
Save therefore I will their lives.
Henceforth, my angel free,

Steer, Strong.

Greet well Noah in this degree ;
Sleeping thou shalt him find.
Bid him go make a ship
Of stiff boards and great ;
Although he be not a wright
Therefore bid him not let.
Bid him in any manner of thing
To ship, when he shall walk,
Of every kind of beast and fowl,
The male and female with him he take.
Bid him go provide, say so,
In ship that they not die,
Take with him hay, corn and straw,
For his fowl and for his fee.

The Angel comes to Noah, and says :
Waken, Noah, to me take heed ;
Noah, if thou hear not this thing
Ever whilst thou live thou shalt repent.

Noah replies : Who art thou, for Heaven's King,
That wakens Noah of his sleeping,
Away I would thou went.

The Angel says : It is an angel to thee sent
To tell thee hard tiding,
For every wight for workës wild,
And many foulëd in sins sore,
And in felony foully filled ;
Therefore a ship thou prepare to steer,
Of true timber highly railed,
With thirty cubits in defence,
Look that she draw when she is dressed ;
And in her side a door thou cut
With windows full fitly set,
And make chambers both more and less
For a flood that shall up burst.
Such a flood in earth shall be
That every life that hath livelihood,

Let, Delay.　　　*Fee*, Cattle.

Beast and body with bone and blood,
They shall be torn through stress of storm,
Save thou, Noah, and thy brood
And their three wivës in your hand ;
For you are full righteous and good,
You shall be safe by sea and land.
Into the ship ere you enter
Take with you both ox and cow.
Of each thing that life has lent,
The male and female take with you.
Fetch in fodder for your freight
To make good purveyance, for you prove
That they perish not in your sight.
Do, Noah, as I have bidden thee now.   [*Exit Angel.*

   Noah replies : Lord, be then in this stead,
That me and mine will save and shield.
For I was never since I was born
Of kind of craft to build a boat.
Christ be the shaper of this ship,
For a ship need make I must.
Now of my work I will begin.   [*Noah goes on build-*
                               ing the ark.

     The Devil enters, and says :

Out, out, harrow, and wel-
    away !
That ever I uprose this day,
So may I smile and say
I went ; there has been none
    alive
Man, beast, child nor wife
But my servants were they.
All this I have heard say,
A ship that made should be
For to save without nay
Noah and his meynee,
Yet trow I, they shall lie.

The Devil.

Meynee, Household.

Thereto make I a vow
To trip them yet I trow,
To Noah's wife will I wend
Make her believe in me ;
In faith she is my friend,
She is both quaint and sly.

Enter Noah's Wife.

Rest well, rest well, my own dear dame !
   Noah's Wife says : Welcome, good sir, what is thy
      name,
Quick that thou tell me.
   The Devil says : To tell my name I were full loth,
I come to warn thee of thy loss ;
I tell thee secretly
If thou do after thy husband's rede
Thou and thy children will all be dead,
And that right hastily.
   Noah's Wife says : Go, devil, how say, for shame !
   The Devil says : Yes, hold thee still, my dame,
Do as I shall bid thee now
Thou shalt know everything.
Have here a drink full good
That is made of a mightful main ;
When he hath drunken a drink of this
No longer shall he learn.
Believe, believe, my own dear dame,
I may no longer bide :
To ship when thou shalt fare,
I shall be at thy side.   *[Exit Devil.*
   Noah says : This labour is full great,
For such an old man as me ;
Lo, lo, fast I sweat
It trickles out at mine ee.
Now homeward will I wend
My weary bones to rest ;

Rede, Counsel, advice.

For such good as God hath sent,
There I get of the best.

    [To his Wife] : Rest well, dame, what cheer with
      thee.

    His Wife says : Welcome, Noah, as I might thrive,
Welcome to thine own wones ;
Sit down here beside me,
Thou hast full weary bones.
Have eaten, Noah, as I might thee,
And soon a drink I shall give thee,
Such drink thou never had before.

    Noah drinks and says : What the devil, what drink
      is it ?
By my father's soul I have near lost my wit.

    His Wife says : Noah, bid you, tell me where you
      about wend,
I give God a vow, we two shall be near friend.

    Noah says : O yes, dame, could thou learn
I would tell thee my wit.
How God of heaven an angel sent
And bade me make a ship :
This world he will fordo
With storms both stiff and fell,
All but thee and me, our children and wives too.

    His Wife says : By my faith I do not reck
Whether thou be friend or foe ;
The devil of hell thee speed
To ship when thou shalt go.

    Noah says : God send me help on high
To clink yon nails to ;
That all may well be done,
My strokes be not in vain.

    The Angel appears and says :
God hath thee help hither sent
Thereof be thou right bold.

    Noah says : Now is the ship well made

Wones, Dwelling.   *I might thee*, I might thrive.

Within and without thinks me :
Now home then will I wend
To fetch in my money.
Have good day, both old and young,
My blessing with you be.

Finis. Amen.

CHAPTER VIII.—THE WAKEFIELD PLAY
OF THE FLOOD

Genesis 6, 7, 8.

As we have pointed out, the earliest of these plays
were performed in one fixed place, such as the market-
place of the town ; but very soon in the larger cities
the custom arose of playing on movable stages,
which could easily be shifted to different places in
the town, where the performance would be repeated.
In this way many more people could see the play. A
writer of the time described one of these stages as " a
high place, made like a house with two rooms, being
open at the top ; in the lower room they apparelled
and dressed themselves, and in the higher room they
played." The whole stage was mounted on wheels
so that it could easily be moved about from place to
place. A number of stations would be chosen, where
the spectators could gather to watch the play. The
first car in the series would present its play at the
first station, and would then move on to the next.
Here the scene would be played over again, whilst
the players on the second car would be giving their
play at the first station. Then both cars would pass
on and the third begin its course, and so on ; so that
the cars arrived at each station in the correct order,
and the audience there would see the play as a con-
tinuous whole.

Needless to say, this required a good deal of organization, and it was usually the business of the town
corporation to see that proper arrangements were

made. At Leicester we read of the appointment of "overseers" and "two beadles" to superintend the production of the play.

It will now be interesting to see how much the original story of Noah had developed at Wakefield when it was played there in the procession of mystery plays. The main outline is still much the same. God speaks from above, and Noah builds his ark at the back of the stage. Noah's wife is by now a perfect character of a noisy and troublesome spouse, who is soundly beaten by her husband. This provides comic relief from the more serious parts of the play, and no doubt the audience welcomed this ludicrous picture of domestic strife. Another interesting difference from the old Cornish play is the way in which the people behave after they have come out of the ark. Noah no longer makes sacrifice, but passes quite ordinary remarks about the destruction caused by the flood. His wife has by now fully quietened down, and the play closes with a prayer of Noah for future protection and salvation.

The Play of Noah and his Sons

God [speaks from above]. Since I have made each
        thing that is alive,
Duke, emperor, and king, with mine own hand,
For to have their liking by sea and by strand ;
Every man to my bidding should bow his head
      Full fervent ;
That made man such a creature,
Fairest of favour,
Who must love me for ever
      By reason, and repent.
Methought I showed man love when I made him
      to be
All angels above, like to the Trinity.
And now in great reproof, full low lies he.

In earth himself to glut with sins that displease me
　　Most of all.
Vengeance will I take
In earth, for sin's sake ;
My anger will I wake
　　Both of great and small.
I repent full sore that ever made I man,
By me he sets no store, by me his sovereign ;
I will destroy therefore both beast, man, and woman,
　　That evil do.
In earth I see right nought
But sin, all unatoned ;
Of those that well have wrought
　　Find I but few.
Therefore shall I fordo all this earth below
With waters that shall flow and rain with hideous
　　roar.
I have good cause thereto ; for me no man hath awe.
As I say, so shall I do ; of vengeance draw my sword
　　And make end
Of all that beareth life,
Save Noah, and his wife ;
For they would never strive
　　With me, nor me offend.
　[God speaks to Noah.] Noah, my friend, I thee
　　command, thy sorrows to dispel,
That thou do make a ship of nail and board full
　　well.
Thou wast e'er a trusty workman, to me as true as
　　steel ;
For thy lasting faithful friendship shalt thou feel
　　Reward.
Of length let thy ship be
Three hundred cubits, warn I thee,
Of height even thirty,
　　And fifty also broad.
Anoint thy ship with pitch and tar, without it and
　　within,

To keep the water out this is a noble gin.
See no man thee hinder : three chief rooms begin.
Thou must use many a beam ere thou thy present
    work
      Shall end fully.
Make in thy ship also
Parlours, one or two,
And other houses, too,
    For beasts therein must be.
When all is done thus right, thy wife, that is thy mate,
    Take in to thee ;
Thy three sons of good fame,
Japhet, Sem and Hame ;
    Their wives also, all three.
For all shall be fordone that live on earth, but ye,
With floods that from above shall fall and that plenty.
It shall begin full soon to rain incessantly,
After seven days more, and lasting full forty,
    Without fail.
Take to thy ship also
Beasts of each kind but two,
Male and female, and no mo,
    Ere thou put up thy sail.
That it may thee avail, when all this is wrought,
Stuff thy ship with victual, for hunger that ye perish
    not ;
Of beasts, fowl, and cattle have thou them in thought ;
For them, is my counsel, that succour be sought
    In haste,
Thou must have corn and hay,
And other meat alway.
Do now as I thee say
    In the name of the Holy Ghost.
  Noah. I thank thee, Lord so dear, that would
    vouchsafe
Thus below to appear to a simple knave ;

Gin, Engine, device.

Bless us, Lord, here ; for charity I it crave,
The better that we may steer the ship that we shall
       have
  Certain.
  God. Noah, to thee and to thy fry
My blessing grant I ;
Ye shall wax and multiply,
    And fill the earth again,
When all these floods are past and fully gone away.
  Noah. Lord, homeward will I haste as fast as I may ;
My wife will I see what she will say.
I am afraid there will be some fray
    Between us both ;
For she is full testy,
For little oft angry ;
If any thing wrong be
    Soon is she wroth.   [*Enter Noah's Wife.*
God-speed, dear wife, how fare ye ?
  Wife. Now, as ever might I thrive, the worse that I
    thee see ;
And tell me now at once where hast thou thus long
    been ?
To death may we drive, or live for thee
    For want
When we sweat or swink,
Thou dost what thou think,
Yet of meat or of drink
    Have we very scant.
  Noah. Wife, we are hard placed with tidings new.
  Wife. Better that thou wert clad in Stafford blue,
For thou art always afraid, be it false or true ;
But God knows, I am led, and that may I rue,
    Full ill.
For I dare be thy pledge,
From evening unto morrow
Thou speakest ever of sorrow ;

Swink, Toil.

God send thee for once thy fill.
We women may curse all ill husbands ;
I have one, by Mary, that should loose me of my
       bands ;
If he be vexed, I must tarry, wringing both my hands
    For rue.
But yet other while,
What with game and with guile,
I shall smite and smile
    And give him his due.

    Noah. Hold thy tongue, ram-skit, or I shall thee
    still.

    Wife. By my thrift, if thou smite, I shall set on thee
    too.

    Noah. I will try quickly.   Have at thee, Jill,
                                    [*He hits her.*
Upon the bone shall it bite.
    Wife.   Ah, so, marry, thou smitest ill,
      But I suppose
I shall not owe thee more
Ere I move from this floor.   [*She hits back.*
    Noah. Ah, wilt thou so ?
    Wife. Thou shalt have three for two, I promise thee
    well.

    Noah. And I shall pay thee out, though it be a sin.

    Wife. Out on thee, ho !

    Noah.   Thou canst both bite and whine
    With great noise ;
But I will keep charity, for much must I do.

    Wife. Here shall no man tarry, I pray thee go to.
To spin will I go now.

    Noah.   Fare thee well, go.
    But, wife,
Pray for me busily
Ere I come back to thee.

    Wife. For all that thou prayest for me,
    Well might I thrive.   [*Exit Wife.*

    Noah. I tarry full long from my work, I trow ;

Now my gear will I fetch and thitherward draw;
I may go full ill, the truth for to know,
But if God help now, I may sit in sorrow
    To see.
Now will I try
How I can do carpentry,
In nomine patris, et filii,
    Et spiritus sancti, Amen.
My gown will I cast, and work in
    my coat.
The mast will I make, ere I stir a
    foot.
My back, I trow, will burst; this
    is a sorry note.
It is a wonder that I last, such an
    old dote,
    All dulled.
To begin such a work
My bones are so stiff,
No wonder if they ache,
    For I am full old.
The top and the sail both will I
    make,
The helm and the castle also will I
    take.
This gear will never fail, that I
    undertake
    Anon.
This is a noble gin;
These nails so they run
Through great and small,
    These boards each one.
Window and door, even as he said,
Three chief chambers that are well
    made,
Pitch and tar full sure thereupon laid,

A Prophet.

(Showing the kind of dress
suitable for Noah.)

In nomine patris, etc., " In the name of the Father, and of the Son,
    and of the Holy Ghost.   Amen."

This will ever endure ; I am satisfied.
　　For why ?
It is better wrought
Than I could have thought.
Him that made all of nought
　　I thank only.
Now will I hie me, that nothing miscarry,
My wife and my household to bring even hither.

[Enter Wife, Sons, and Sons' Wives.

Take heed in good time, wife, and consider ;
Hence must we flee one with another
　　In haste.

　Wife. Why, sir, what ails you ?
What is that which assails you ?
To flee will avail you
　　If you be aghast.

　Noah. He that cares may kill, blest be his name !
Has for our safety, to shield us from shame,
　　Foretold
All this world about,
With waters so stout
That shall run in a rout
　　Shall be overlaid.
He said all shall be slain, save us alone,
Our bairns so obedient, and their wivës three.
A ship he bade me fashion, to save us and our goods ;
Therefore with all our house thank we his grace,
　　The healer of ill.
Hie us fast ; go we hither.

　Wife. I know not whither ;
I am dazed and I dither
　　For fear at thy tale.

　Noah. Be not afraid ; have done ; pack up our gear.

　First Son. It shall full soon be done. Brother,
　　help me to bear.

　Second Son. I shall not long tarry, but take my
　　share,
　　　Brother Sem.

Third Son. Without any boast now
With my might shall I help you.
    Wife. Yet for fear that she beat you
      Help well thy dame.
    Noah. Now we are there, as we should be,
Get in our gear, goods and cattle,
In this vessel here, my children free.
    Wife. Sir, nor for Jack nor for Jill, will I turn my
      face
Till I have on this hill spun a space
      On my distaff.
Now will I down set me,
Yet rede I no man let me,
      For fear of a knock.
    Noah. Behold in the heaven, the cataracts all
That are open full even, great and small.
And the planets seven have left their place ;
These thunders and lightning will cause the downfall
      Full stout
Of both halls and bowers,
Castles and towers.
Full sharp are these showers
      That rain all about.
Therefore, wife, have done, come into ship fast.
    Wife. In faith, yet will I spin ;
      All in vain ye carp.
    Third Son's Wife. If you like you may spin, mother,
      in the ship.
    Noah. Now come thee in, dame, on my friendship.
    Wife. Whether I lose or I win now thy fellowship
I care not a pin ; this spindle I slip
      Upon this hill
Ere I stir one foot.
    Noah. Peter ! I trow we dote.
Without any more note
      Come in if ye will.

Rede, Advise.   **Let**, Hinder.

Wife. Yea, the water comes so near, that I sit not
    dry,
Into the ship quickly therefore will I hie,
For dread that I drown here.
    Noah.   Dame, surely
It hath cost full dear, ye abode so long by
    Out of ship.
    Wife. I will not do thy bidding.
    Noah. In faith, for your long tarrying
    You shall taste of the whip.
    Wife. Spare me not, I pray thee, do even as you
    think ;
Thy great words shall not flay me.   [*Noah beats her.*
    Noah.   Abide, dame, and drink ;
For beaten thou shalt be with this staff till thou stink.
Are my strokes good ?   Tell me ?
    Wife.   What say you, Wat Wynk ?
    Noah. Speak.
Cry me mercy, I say.
    Wife. Thereto say I nay.
    Noah. If thou dost not, by this day,
    Thy head shall I break.
    Wife. Lord, would I be easy, and full of good cheer,
Might I have but one meal of true widow's fare ;
For thy soul, without loss, would I pay for a prayer.
So would others, no doubt, that I see in this place
    Of wives that are here.
For the lives that they lead
Wish their husbands were dead,
For, as e'er I eat bread,
    I would so our sire were.
    Noah. Ye men that have wives ; whilst they are
    young,
If you love but your lives, chastise their tongue.
    Wife. Yet may you suffer,
    Nicoll Neddy !
    Noah. I shall make you as still as a stone, beginner
    of blunder !

I shall beat thy back and bone, and break all in
      sunder.   *[He beats her.*

   Wife. Out alas I am gone ! out upon thee, man's
      wonder !

   Noah. See how she can groan, and I lie under !
      But wife,

In this last let us stay,

For my back is near in two.

   Wife. I am beaten so blue
      That I may not recover.

   First Son. Ah, why fare ye thus ? father and
      mother both !

   Second Son. Ye should not be so spiteful, standing
      in a wroth.

   Noah. We will do as ye bid us, we will no more be
      wroth,

     Dear bairns.   *[They all go into the ark.*

But now to the helm will I bend

And my ship tend.

   Wife. I see in the firmament,
      Methink, the seven stars.

   Noah. This is a great flood, wife, take heed.

   Wife. So methought, as I stood ; we are in great
      dread,

The waves are so wild.

   Noah.   Help, God, in this need

As thou art steersman good, and best as I rede,

     Of all ;

Guide us now in this flood,

As thou didst me promise.

   Wife. This is a parlous case ;
      Help, God, when we call !

   Noah. Wife, take the steer-tree, and I will assay

The depth of the sea to test if I may.

   Wife. That shall I do full wisely ; now go thy way,

For upon this flood have we sailed many a day

     With sorrow.

   Noah. Now the water will I sound.

   (2,753)

Ah! It is far to the ground.
This labour I expound
   Had I to lose.
Above all this at once, the water is risen late
Cubits fifteen, but in a higher state
It may not be, I ween, for this well I know,
That forty days has rain been; it will therefore abate
   Full sure.
This water in haste,
Again will I try;
Now am I aghast
   It has waned a great deal.
Now are the waters ceased and the cataracts stayed,
Both the most and the least.

   Wife. Methink, by my wit,
The sun shines in the east; is not yonder it?
We should have a good feast were these floods gone,
   So spiteful.

   Noah. We have been here, all we,
Three hundred days and fifty.

   Wife. Yea, now wanes the sea,
   Lord, well is us!

   Noah. The third time will I prove what deepness we
   bear.

   Wife. Now long shall thou delay, lay in thy line there.

   Noah. I may touch with my hoof the ground even
   here.

   Wife. Then begins to grow with us merry cheer;
   But, husband,
What ground may this be?

   Noah. The hills of Armenye.

   Wife. Now blessed be he
   That thus for us hath ordained.

   Noah. I see tops of hills here, many at a sight,
Nothing to delay me, the weather is so bright.

   Wife. There are of mercy tokens full right.

   Noah. Dame, thy counsel; what fowl best might,
   And could

With flight of wing
Bring, without tarrying,
Of mercy some tokening
  Either by north or south ?
For this is the first day of the tenth month.
 Wife. The raven durst I lay will come again soon.
As fast as thou canst cast him forth, have done.
He may haply to-day come again or none
  With favour.
 Noah. I will cast out also
Doves, one or two.
Go your way, go.
  God send you some prey
Now are these fowl flown into far country,
Pray we fast, each one, kneeling on our knee,
To him that is alone worthiest of degree,
That he will send anon our fowls something
  To glad us.
 Wife. They may not fail of land,
The water is so waning.
 Noah. Thank we God Almighty,
  The Lord that made us.
It is a wondrous thing, methink soothly
They are so long tarrying, the fowls, that we
Cast out in the morning.
 Wife.   Sir, it may be
They tarry till they bring.
 Noah.   The raven is an-hungry
  Alway ;
He is without any reason ;
If he find no carrion,
As peradventure may befall,
  He will not away.
The dove is more gentle, her trust I unto,
Like unto the turtle, for she is ay true.
 Wife. Here but a little she comes. Lew, lew !
She brings in her bill some novel new.
  Behold !

It is of an olive tree
A branch thinks me.

    Noah. It is so, perdie,
    Right so is it called.

Dove, bird full blest, fair might thee befall !
Thou art as true for to trust as stone in the wall ;
Full well it I wist, thou would come to thy hall.

    Wife. A true token it is, we shall be saved all.
    For why ?

The water since she came
Is fallen a fathom
    And more, hardly.

    First Son. These floods are gone—father, behold.
    Second Son. There is left right none, and so be ye bold.
    Third Son. As still as a stone our ship is set.
    Noah. Upon land here anon that we were, fain I
        would.

My children dear,
Sem, Japhet, and Hame,
With glee and with game,
Come we together ;
    We will no longer abide here.

    Wife. Here have we been nigh long enow,
With sorrow and grief, dread and much woe.

    Noah. Behold on this green neither cart nor plough
Is left, as I ween, neither tree nor bough,
    Nor other thing.

But all is away.
Many castles, I say,
Great towns of array
    Destroyed has this flowing.

To death are they dight, proudest of pride,
Every creature that ever was spied
    With sin.

All are they slain
And put into pain.

    Wife. From thence again
    May they never come ?

Noah. Come ? No, in faith ; but he that might has
Would remember their sorrow and admit them to
     grace.
As he in affliction is comfort, I pray him in this space,
In heaven high with his own, to give us a place ;
    That we
With his saints in sight,
And his angels bright,
May come to his light.
    Amen, for charity.

CHAPTER IX.—THE COVENTRY PLAY OF
Genesis 1, 2, 3   THE CREATION

THE players in the Mysteries did not perform solely
for the sheer joy of acting in public. The plays were
looked upon as part of the corporate life of the town,
and the authorities were naturally anxious to keep up
the standard of performance, as badly produced plays
would be bad for their reputation. Hence it became
usual for the players to receive some sort of salary for
their performance, and fines were also in force if a gild
did not do its scene well enough. A number of accounts of payments of this sort, and of payments for
the cost of production, have been saved. At Coventry,
in 1439, the authorities ordered " that every craft have
pageant to play in, that the pageant be made ready
and brought forth to play upon pain of 100s., to be
raised by the iiij masters of the crafts that so offend."
At Beverley (Yorkshire), in 1452, Henry Cowper, a
weaver, was fined 6s. 8d. for not knowing his part,
whilst about seventy years later the entire gild of
painters got into very hot water for the bad production
of their play: (At this time a shilling was worth con-
siderably more than it is now. Sixpence a day was
considered the usual wage for a town workman—the
kind of man who took part in the mystery play.)

Payments of actors are also recorded. At Hull the man who played Noah received 1s., but at Coventry the rates were higher. Pilate got 5s., Caiaphas and Annas, and the two Maries, 1s. apiece. A soul, whether it was represented as saved or damned, was paid 1s. 8d., and a demon 1s. 4d. Drink for the players of the Coventry Cappers, consumed between the play times, cost 1s. 1d., whilst in the same town a man named Fawston earned 4d. for imitating the cock crowing, presumably in the scene of Peter's denial. Another man got 4d. "for keeping of fire at hell mouth."

The cost of producing the plays is equally interesting. We find a Coventry record of the making of scenery :

Item, paid for linen cloth to paint .   5s. 0d.
Item, paid to Horseley the painter.   23s. 4d.

We have seen in the plays of the Flood how God was represented as sitting above in glory, and in this town 12d. was spent on obtaining his throne. The provision of an actor's clothes is recorded also :

Item, paid for the Demon's garment and
    making the stuff .   .   .   .   . 5s. 3½d.
Item, paid for colouring of the same gar-
    ment   .   .   .   . 8d.

But the real pride of the Coventry players was their staging of the End of the World in the Scene of the Doomesday, in which the Drapers produced a "yerthequake" at a cost of 3s. 4d. A man received what we have seen to be the usual payment for stage-hands, 4d. "for attending the earthquake." The destruction of the world by fire seems also to have been represented, and as one world had to be destroyed at each performance, a single one was not enough, so we hear of 2s. being "paid to Crowe for making of three worlds." There is also the quaint entry : "Paid for setting the world on fire, 5*d*." But perhaps the most delightful of all the Coventry payments was 2*s*. 6*d*. " to John Dean for taking pains about the pageant."

Coventry, where all these records survive, has the unique honour of two recorded sets of plays. There is the usual gild series, of which we shall later on read the *Taylors and Shearmen's Play of the Nativity*. Besides this, of which two plays have survived, there is a complete set entitled *Ludus Coventræ* [in English, *The Play of Coventry*], or *The Play of Corpus Christi*, as it is sometimes called. Many eminent scholars have tried to solve the problem of this second series of plays. There is a tempting theory that they were performed in various parts of the Midlands by strolling players, whose headquarters may have been at Coventry. Some authorities suggest that they were acted by the Franciscan Friars of Coventry, who took them, as we should say, "on tour." If this is true, we have here something different from the plays of the craft gilds—plays which were performed by men of a religious body for the purpose of spreading the knowledge of the Bible stories. But we must accept with caution suppositions of this kind, although it seems hardly possible that a town of the size of Coventry should have two complete series of plays on Corpus Christi Day. We must also remember that the accounts of payments we have just been studying belong to the gildsmen's plays.

The Creation

God speaks. Ego sum Alpha et Omega, principium
    et finis.
My name is known, God and king,

Ego sum . . . finis, "I am Alpha and Omega, the beginning and the end." *Alpha* and *Omega* are the first and last letters of the Greek alphabet.

My work for to make now will I wend.
In myself resteth my reigning,
It hath no beginning nor no end,
It is closèd in my mind
When it is made at my liking;
I may it save, I may destroy,
After my pleasure.
So great of might is my power

All things shall be wrought by me.
I am one God in persons three
Knit in one substance.
I am the true Trinity
Here walking in this one,
Three persons myself I see
Locked in me, God alone;
I am father of might,
My son kept right,
My ghost had light
And grace withal.
Myself beginning never did take,
And endless I am through my own
      might;
Now will I begin my work to make:
First I make heaven with stars of light
In mirth and joy evermore to wake.
In heaven I build angels full bright
My servants to be, and for my sake
With mirth and melody worship my
      might;

An Angel.

I build them in my bliss.
Angels in heaven evermore shall be
With mirth and song to worship me
Of joys they may not miss.

Here the angels sing in heaven. "To thee all angels, to thee the heavens and all the powers therein, to thee cherubim and seraphim continually do cry: Holy, holy, holy, lord God of Sabaoth."

Enter Lucifer, who says:

To whose worship sing ye this song?
To worship God or reverence me?
Unless ye me worship, ye do me wrong,
For I am the worthiest that ever may be.

   The Good Angels. We worship God, of might most
       strong,
Who hath formed both us and thee,
We can never worship him too long,
For he is most worth of majesty.
On our knees to God we fall,
Our lord God worship we,
A greater lord may never there be
Than he that made us all.

   Lucifer. A worthier lord, forsooth am I
And worthier than he, even will I be.
In evidence that I am more worthy
I will go sit me in God's see.
Above sun and moon and stars in sky
I am now set, as ye may see.
Now worship me for most mighty
And for your lord honour now me
Sitting in my seat.

   The Bad Angels. God's might we forsake
And for more worthy we thee take
And fall down at thy feet.

   God. Thou, Lucifer, for thy much pride
I bid thee fall from heaven to hell;
And all that hold them on thy side
In my bliss never more to dwell.
At my commandment anon down thou slide,
With mirth and joy never more to share;
In mischief and menace ever shalt thou abide
In bitter burning and fire so fell.

   Lucifer. At thy bidding thy will I do
And pass from joy to painës smart;

See, Seat, a word still used in speaking of a bishop's see.

Now I am a devil full dark,
That was an angel bright.
Now to hell the way I take
In endless pain there to be put ;
In hell's dungeon my den is dight.

> [*He goes out, with the Bad Angels.*

   God. Now heaven is made for angels' sake,
The first day and the first night ;
The second day, water I make,
The welkin also full fair and bright.
The third day, I part water from earth,
Tree and every growing thing,
Both herb and flower of sweet smelling,
The third day is made by my working.
Now make I the day that shall be the fourth.
Sun and moon and stars also,
The fourth day, I make the same ;
The fifth day worm and fish that swim and go.
And I make thee, man, Adam by name ;
In earthly paradise without woe
I grant thee dwelling, unless thou sin :
Flesh of thy flesh, and bone of thy bone
Adam here is thy wife and mate.
Both fish and fowls that swim and go,
For each of them a name thou take ;
Both tree and fruit and beasts each one,
Red and white, both blue and black,
Thou give them name by thyself alone
Herbs and grass, both plants and brake ;
Thy wife thou give name also.
Look that ye not cease
Your fruit to increase,
That there may be press
Me worship to do.
Now come forth Adam to paradise,
There shalt thou have all manner thing ;
Both flesh and fish and fruit of price

Press, A crowd of people, throng.

All shall be ready at this bidding.
Here is pepper, spice, and sweet liquorice,
Take them all at thy liking,
Both apple and pear and gentle rice,
But touch not this tree that is of Knowledge ;
All things save this for thee are wrought.
Here are all things that thee should please,
All ready made unto thine ease.
Eat not this fruit, nor me displease,
For then thou diest ; thou escapest not.
Now have I made all things of nought,
Heaven and earth, fowl and beast——
To all things that my hand hath wrought,
I grant my blessing that ever shall last.
My way to heaven is ready, sooth,
Of working I will the seventh day rest,
And all my creatures that be about
My blessing ye shall have both east and west.
Of working the seventh day ye cease,
Of all them that cease from labour here
The seventh day, without fear,
And worship me in good manner,
They shall in heaven have endless peace.
Adam go forth and be prince in this place,
For to heaven I speed my way.
Thy wits well look thou chase,
And ghostly govern thee, as I say.

The Fall of Man

Paradise. Enter Adam and Eve.

Adam. Holy father, blessed thou be,
For I may walk in riches now,
I find days great plenty
And many fruits on every bough ;
All this wealth is given to me,

Chase, Govern, order.

And to my wife, who me doth love.
I have no need to touch yon tree,
Against my lord's will to work now,
I am a good gardener.
Every fruit of rich name
I may gather in with glee and mirth ;
To break the trust I were to blame
That my lord bade me keep here.

   Eve. We may be both blithe and glad,
Our lord's commandment to fulfil ;
With many fruits be we fair fed,
Wonder sweet and never one ill.
Every tree with fruit is spread,
Of them to take, as pleaseth us ;
Our wits would be hasty and overwrought,
To forfeit against our lord's will
In any wise.   *[Adam goes out into the garden.*
In this garden I will go see
All the flowers of fair beauty,
And taste the fruits of great plenty,
That be in paradise.

Enter the Serpent.

   Serpent. Hail, fair wife and comely dame !
This fruit to eat I thee counsel ;
Take this apple and eat this same ;
This fruit is best as I thee tell.

   Eve. That apple to eat I were to blame,
From joy our Lord would us expel ;
We should die and be put out with shame,
In joy of paradise never more to dwell.
God himself thus said ;
What day of that fruit we eat,
With these words did God make threat
That we should die, our life to lose ;
Therefore I am afraid.

   Serpent. Of this apple if ye will bite,
Even as God is, so shall ye be,

Wise of knowledge, I promise you,
Like unto God in all degree.
Sun and moon and stars bright,
Flesh and fowl, both send and see,
At your bidding both day and night.
All things shall be in your power ;
Ye shall be God's peer.
Take this apple in thy hand
And bite thereof thou try ;
Take another to thy husband,
Thereof have thou no fear.

   Eve. So wise as God is in his great might,
And equal in knowledge fain would I be.

   Serpent. Eat this apple, and in certain
That I am true, soon shalt thou see.

   Eve. To mine husband with heart full fain
This apple I bear as thou biddest me.   [*Exit Serpent.*
This fruit to eat I shall assay
So wise as God is, that we truly be,
And God's equal in might.
To my husband I walk my way,
And of this apple I shall assay
To make him to eat, if that I may
And of this fruit to bite.

Enter Adam.

My seemly spouse and good husband,
Listen to me, sir, I you pray ;
Take this fair apple in your hand
Thereof a morsel bite and taste.
To eat this apple, if but ye try,
God's equal to be always,
All his wisdom to understand,
And God's own peer to be alway,
All things for to make——
Both fish and fowl, see and send,
Bird and beast, water and land ;
Thy apple thou take out of my hand,

A bite thereof thou take.

    Adam. I dare not touch thine hand for dread
Of our Lord God omnipotent,
If I should follow thy counsel
By God, our maker, I should be cursed.
If that we do this sinful deed,
We shall be dead by God's judgment.
Out of thine hand with hasty speed,
Cast out that apple at once present
For fear of God's great threat.

    Eve. Of this apple if thou wilt bite,
God's equal shalt thou become
So wise of knowledge, I promise thee,
This fruit if thou wilt eat.

    Adam. If it we eat ourselves we kill,
As God told us we should be dead ;
To eat that fruit and my life to lose
I dare not follow thy counsel.

    Eve. A fair angel hath told me thus :
" To eat this apple be never so dread,
So wise as God on heaven's high hill
Thou shalt be soon, within a space ;
Therefore this fruit thou eat."

    Adam. Of God's great wisdom for to learn,
And in wisdom to be his peer,
Of thine hand I take it here,
And shall soon taste this meat.

*They eat of their apples ; and God approaches from on
    high. With newly-found shame they run to hide
    themselves. God speaks :*

Adam, that with mine hands I made,
Where art thou now ? What hast thou wrought ?

    Adam. Ah, Lord ! For sin our flowers do fade ;
I hear thy voice, but I see thee not.

    God. Adam, why hast thou sinned so soon,
Thus hastily to break my boon,
And I made thee master, under none,

Truly of every tree.
One tree I kept for mine own,
Life and death therein I know :
Thy sin from life now thee hath thrown,
From death thou mayst not flee.

    Adam. Lord, I have wrought against thy will
I spared not myself to spill ;
This woman thou took me to
She brought me thereto.
It was her counsel and advice ;
She bade me do the same deed.
I walk as a worm without a garment,
I have no shroud nor shoe.

    God. Woman, that art this man's wife,
Why hast thou stirred up for both strife ?
Now ye be from your fair life,
And are deemed for to die.
Unwise woman, tell me why,
That thou hast done this foul folly,
And I made thee a great lady,
In paradise for to play.

    Eve. Lord ! when thou wentest from this place,
A worm, which had an angel's face,
He bade us to be full of grace,
The fruit if that we ate.
I did his bidding, alas, alas,
I suppose it was Sathanas
To pain he would us put.   *[The Serpent appears.*

    God [to the Serpent] : Thou worm, with thy will so weak,
Thy false stories they be full thick,
Why hast thou put death's prick
On Adam and his wife ?
In hell's house thou shalt be locked
And never more latch lift.

    The Serpent. I shall thee tell wherefore and why

Spill, Destroy, cause to perish.

I did him all this villainy,
For I am full of great envy,
Of wrath and wicked hate ;
That man should live above the sky
Where as sometime dwelt I,
And now I am cast to hell's sty
Straight out of heaven's gate.

　　God. Adam ! for thou that apple bit,
Against my bidding, well I wot,
Go earn thy meat with swink and sweat
Unto thy life's end.
Go naked, hungry, and barefoot,
Eat both herbs and grass and root,
Thy sin deserves no other meed,
As wretched on earth thou wend.
Woman that caused this sinning
And bade him break my bidding,
Therefore be thou his underling,
To man's bidding bend,
Unto thy life's end.

　　[*To the Serpent*] : Thou wicked worm full of pride,
Foul envy sit by thy side,
Upon thy belly thou shalt glide,
A worm wicked in wit.
Until a maiden in earth be born,
Thou fiend I warn thee before,
Through her thy foul head shall be torn,
Crawling, away go thou.

　　The Devil. At thy bidding foul I fall,
I creep home to my stinking stall ;
Hell's pit and heaven's hall
Shalt do thy bidding fair.
I fall down here, a foul fellow,
For this fall begin to quake
My sorrow cometh full soon.　　　　　[*Exit Serpent.*

　　God. For your sin that ye have done,
Out of this bliss soon shall ye go,
In earthly labour to live in woe

And sorrow ye shall taste.
For your sin and misdoing,
An angel with a sword burning
Out of this joy he shall you drive,
Your wealth away is passed.

*God returns to heaven, and an angel seraph with a
    flaming sword drives Adam and Eve from Paradise.*

 Seraph. Ye wretches unknowing, and right unwise,
Of this joy live you in haste;
With flaming sword from paradise
To pain I beat you, of care to taste.
Your mirth is turned to woeful sighs,
Your wealth with sin away is waste,
For your false deed of sinful kind,
This bliss I shut from you right fast.
Herein come ye no more,
Till a child of a maid be born,
And upon the cross be rent and torn,
To save all whom ye have forlorn,
Your wealth for to restore.
 Adam. Now let us walk forth into the land,
With right great labour our food to find,
With delving and digging with mine hand,
Our bliss to bale and care wasted.
And, wife, to spin must thou now try,
Our naked bodies in clothes to wrap,
Till some comfort of God's sending,
With grace relieve our careful mind;
Now come, go we hence, wife.
 Eve. Alas! that ever we wrought this sin;
Our bodily sustenance for to win,
You must delve and I shall spin,
In care to lead our life.
                    [*They are driven out by the Angel.*

CHAPTER X.—THE PROPHETS

IN the very early days, when the tropes were still only
just becoming transformed into simple plays, one very
favourite incident was a procession of the prophets of
the Old Testament. Each of them in turn would bear
witness of the coming of the Messiah. Naturally they
are also to be found in the miracle plays ; and in the
Play of Coventry, from which the following brief selection has been made, each prophet is accompanied by
a king of the House of Judah. There is very little
opportunity for elaborate acting in a scene like this,
in which the prophets and kings make their speeches
of prophecy in order of importance, beginning with
Isaiah, Jesse, and King David.

The Prophets

Isaiah the Prophet. I am the prophet called Ysaie,
Replete with God's great influence,
And say plainly, with spirit of prophecy,
That a pure maid, through meek obedience
Shall bear a child which shall do resistance
Against foul Zabulon, the devil of hell,
Man's soul against him to defend ;
Open in the field the fiend he shall fell.
Our life for to save he shall suffer death
And buy us to his bliss in heaven for to dwell
Of sacerdotal lineage ; the truth I you tell.
Flesh and blood to take, God will be born ;
Joy to man on earth, and in heaven angels
At the child's birth joy shall make that morn.
  Jesse. A blessed branch shall spring of me
That shall be sweeter than balm's breath ;
Out of that branch in Nazareth
A flower shall bloom of me, Jesse the root,
The which by grace shall destroy death

And bring mankind to bliss most sweet.

David the King. I am David, of Jesse's root,
The fresh king by natural succession,
And of my blood shall spring our saviour,
As God himself hath made promis-
     sion.

Jeremiah the Prophet. I am the
     prophet Jeremy,
And full accord in all sentence
With King David and with Ysaie,
Affirming plainly before this audi-
     ence
That God of his high benevolence
Of priest and king will take lineage
And buy us all from our offence
In heaven to have his heritage.

Solomon the King. I am Solomon
     the second king,
And that worthy temple forsooth
     made I ;
Which is the symbol of that maid
     young
That shall be mother of great
     Messiah.

Ezekiel the Prophet. A vision of
     this full verily
I, Ezekiel, have had also
Of a gate that barred was truly
And no man but a prince might
     therein go.

Asa the King. I, King Asa, be-
     lieve all this,
That God will of a maiden be born
And, us to bring to endless bliss,
Rudely on cross be rent and torn.

Jonah the Prophet. I, Jonah, say that on the third
     morn
From death he shall rise, this is a true tale ;

Joel.

(Showing the kind of dress
suitable for a prophet.)

Figured in me, who long before
Lay three days buried within the whale.
   Amon the King. Amon, king, for the last conclusion
All things before said for truth do testify ;
Pray that Lord, of our sins' remission
At that dreadful day he grant us mercy.
Thus we all of this genealogy
According in one, here in this place
Pray that high lord, when that we shall die
Of his great goodness to grant us his grace.

CHAPTER XI.—THE PAGEANT OF SHEARMEN AND TAYLORS

WE now come to our one play from the craft gilds of
Coventry, the story of the Birth of our Lord as performed by the Taylors and Shearmen. We have
already heard a good deal about the organization of
the plays of this town, and we find further evidence
of their wide reputation in the *Hundred Merry Tales*,
a book published in 1526, in which a preacher tells his
congregation : " If ye believe not me, then for more
surety and sufficient authority, go your way to
Coventry, and there ye shall see them all played in
Corpus Christi Play."

   This play tells a very composite story of the An-
nunciation, the coming of the Shepherds and of the
Three Kings, of Herod and the Slaying of the Children.
As a play it is still a little clumsy. The tale rambles
on without much regard for the correct proportions
of the story.

   Just as Noah's wife became a figure of fun, so here
we find Herod changed into a swaggering bully who
rages in fury when things do not go as he wishes.
Shakespeare, who lived not far from Coventry, knew
of this tradition of a swaggering Herod, for we find
Hamlet tells the Players how he would " have such

a fellow whipped for o'erdoing Termagant; it out-
herods Herod; pray you avoid it." Moreover, for
the benefit of these audiences of simple folk it became
necessary to make the characters as obvious as
possible, and so Herod always raged, and usually wore
a helmet and a blue satin gown. It also became
customary to treat him as a Saracen warrior, and he
always swears by Mahound, who of course, in the days
of the real Herod, was not yet born. The Devil also
had his style. He would often appear in a suit of
black leather wielding a large club, and almost in-
variably began his first speech with " Ho, ho, ho ! "
or else with " Out, harrow ! "

Another common trick of this kind was to represent
Cain and very often Judas Iscariot with a fierce tawny
coloured beard and whiskers, and this is no doubt
what Shakespeare was thinking of when he speaks of
" Cain-coloured " as meaning red or tawny coloured.
In the works of the same poet is recorded another
tradition about Cain being made to slay his brother
with an old jawbone, much as Samson slew the
Philistines. Hamlet points out to Horatio how the
Gravedigger beats on the ground with the skull he
has just found, " as if it were Cain's jawbone that did
the first murder."

The Pageant of Shearmen and Taylors

Enter Isaiah for the Prologue.

Isaiah. The Sovereign that seeth every secret,
He save you all, and make you perfect and strong,
And give us grace with his mercy for to meet !
For now in great measure mankind is bound.
The serpent hath given us so mortal a wound,
That no creature is able us for to release,

Termagant, A violent tyrant sometimes represented in these plays,
    and apparently imagined to be a Saracen god.

Till thy right unction of Judah doth cease.
Then shall much mirth and joy increase,
And the right root in Israel spring,
That shall bring forth the grain of wholeness ;
And out of danger he shall us bring
Into that region where he is king,
Which above all other far doth abound ;
And that cruel Satan he shall confound.
Wherefore I come here upon this ground,
To comfort every creature of birth ;
For I, Isaiah the prophet, have found
Many sweet matters whereof we may make mirth,
In this same wise :
For though that Adam be deemed to death,
With all his children, as Abel and Seth,
Lo, where a remedy shall rise.
Behold, a maid shall conceive a child
And get us more grace than ever man had.
His glorious birth shall redeem man again
From bondage and thrall.
More of this matter fain would I tell,
But longer time have I not here for to dwell.
The Lord, that is merciful, his mercy soon in us may
        prove,
For to save our souls from the darkness of hell,
And to his bliss he us bring, as he is both lord and king,
And shall be everlasting *in sæcula sæculorum*, Amen.
                                    [*Exit Isaiah.*

*Enter the Virgin Mary, and, to meet her, the Angel
            Gabriel.*

  Gabriel. Hail, Mary, full of grace, our Lord God is
        with thee ;
Above all women that ever was,
Lady, blessed may thou be.
  Mary. Almighty father, and king of bliss,
From all disease thou save me now,

        In sæcula sæculorum, " For ever and ever."

For inwardly my spirit troubled is,
That I am amazed and know not how.
   Gabriel. Dread thee nothing, maiden, of this;
From heaven above hither am I
     sent
On embassage from that king of
     bliss
Unto thee, lady and virgin reverent,
Saluting thee here as most excel-
     lent,
Whose virtue above all other doth
     abound.
The Holy Ghost on thee shall light,
And shadow thy soul soon with
     virtue
From the Father, that is on height;
These words, fair maid, they be
     full true:
This child that of thee shall be born
Is the Second Person in Trinity,
He shall save that was forlorn,
And the fiend's power destroy shall
     he.
   Mary. Now that it be that Lord's
     will
His high pleasures for to fulfil,
As his one handmaid I submit me.
   Gabriel. Now fare well, Lady, of
     mighty most,
Unto the godhead I thee commit.
   Mary. That Lord thee guide in
   ·   every place,
And lowly he lead me, my saviour he.

An Old Man.

(Isaiah and Joseph should
be dressed in this style.)

*Here the Angel departeth, and Joseph cometh in and
saith:*

Mary, my wife so dear,
How do you do, dame, and what cheer

Is with you this tide ?

Mary. Truly, husband, I am here,
Our Lord's will for to abide.

Joseph. Now to Bethlehem must I wend,
And show myself so full of care ;
Were I to leave us thus far behind,
God wot the while, dame, how you should fare.

Mary. Nay hardly, husband, dread ye nothing,
For I will walk with you on the way ;
I trust in God, almighty king,
To speed right well our journey.

Joseph. Now I thank you, Mary, of your goodness,
That ye my words will not blame ;
And since to Bethlehem we shall us dress,
Go we together in God's holy name.

[*They set out, and travel, as it were, to Bethlehem.*

Now to Bethlehem have we leagues three,
The day is nigh spent, it draweth toward night ;
Fain at your ease, dame, I would you should be,
For you grow all weary, it seemeth in my sight.

Mary. Unto some place, Joseph, kindly me lead,
That I might rest me with grace in this tide.

Joseph. Lo, blessed Mary, here shall ye stay,
And for help to town will I wend.
Is not this the best, dame ? what say ye ?

Mary. God have mercy, Joseph, my husband so meek,
And heartily I pray you, go now from me.

Joseph. That shall be done in haste, Mary, so sweet.
[*Joseph goes out on one side as to Bethlehem ; Mary goes
    out on the other to await his return.*

Enter a Shepherd.

First Shepherd. Now, God, that art in Trinity,
Thou save my fellows and me ;
For I know not where my sheep nor they be
This night, it is so cold.
Now it is nigh the midst of the night ;
This weather is dark and dim of light,

That of them can I have no sight,
Standing here on this wold.
But now to make their hearts light
Now will I full right stand upon this hill,
And to them cry with all my might,
Full well my voice they know—
What ho, fellows, ho, hoo, ho.

Enter two other Shepherds.

Second Shepherd. Hark, Sim, hark! I hear our
    brother on the hill,
This is his voice; right well I know;
Therefore toward him let us go,
And follow his voice aright.
See, Sim, see where he doth stand,
I am right glad we have him found.
Brother, where hast thou been so long,
And this night it is so cold.

First Shepherd. Eh! friends, there came a gust of
    wind with a mist suddenly,
That forth, off my way, went I,
And was full sore afraid.
Then for to go wist I not whither,
But travelled on this hill, hither and thither.
I was so weary of this cold weather
That near passed was my might.

Third Shepherd. Brother, now we be past that fright,
And it is far into the night,
Full soon will spring the day light,
It draweth full near the tide.
Here awhile let us rest,
Till that the sun rise in the east,
Let us all here abide.

*Then the Shepherds draw forth their meat, and do eat
    and drink, and as they drink they see the star, and
    say thus :*

Third Shepherd. Brother, look up and behold,

What thing is yonder, that shineth so bright?
As long as ever I have watched my fold,
Yet never saw I such a sight in field.
Aha! Now is come the time that old fathers have told,
That in the winter's night so cold,
A child of maiden born be he would
In whom all prophecies shall be fulfilled.

    First Shepherd. Truth it is without nay,
So saith the prophet Isaye;
That a child should be born of a maid so bright,
In winter, nigh the shortest day,
Or else in the middest of the night.

    Second Shepherd. Loved be God, most of might,
That our grace is to see that sight;
Pray we to him as it is right,
If that his will it be.
That we may have knowledge of this signification,
And why it appeareth in this fashion;
And ever to him let us give laudation,
In earth while that we be.

       [*Here the Angels sing, " Gloria in excelsis Deo."*

    Third Shepherd. Hark! They sing above in the
        clouds clear;
Hear I never of so sweet a quire;
Now, gentle brother, draw we near
To hear their harmony.

    First Shepherd. Brother, mirth and solace is come
        us among,
For by the sweetness of their song
God's son is come, whom we have looked for long;
As signifieth this star that we do see.

    Second Shepherd. " Glore, gloria in excelsis," that
        was their song;
How say ye, fellows, said they not thus?

    First Shepherd. That is well said; now go we hence,
To worship that child of high magnificence,

    Gloria in excelsis Deo, " Glory to God in the Highest."

And that we may sing in his presence,
" Et in terra pax omnibus."

Angels appear to the Shepherds.

First Angel. Shepherds fair, dread ye nothing
        Of this star that ye do see ;
        For this same morn, God's son is born
        In Bethlehem, of a maiden free.
Second Angel. Hie you thither in haste ;
        It is his will ye shall him see
        Lying in a crib, of poor repast ;
        Yet of David's line come is he.

*The Angels disappear. The Shepherds go out as on
    their way to Bethlehem, singing :*

As I out rode this passing night,
Of three jolly shepherds I saw a sight ;
And all about their fold, a star shone bright.
    They sang terly terlow
    So merrily the shepherds their pipes can blow.

*The scene changes to the manger, where are Mary and
    Joseph with the Child. Enter the Shepherds, who
    come and kneel before the Child.*

First Shepherd. Hail ! Maid, mother, and wife so
        mild,
As the angel saith, so have we found :
I have nothing to present to thy child
But my pipe ; hold, hold, take it in thy hand,
Wherein much pleasure that I have found.
And now to honour thy glorious birth,
Thou shall it have to make thee mirth.
    Second Shepherd. Now hail be thou, child, and thy
        dame,
For in a poor lodging here thou art laid :
So the angel said and told us thy name.

Et in terra pax omnibus, "And on earth peace unto all men."

Hold, take thou here my hat on thy head,
And now of one thing thou art well sped ;
Of weather thou hast no need to complain,
Of wind, nor sun, hail, snow, and rain.

    Third Shepherd. Hail be thou, lord over water and
        lands ;
For thy coming all we may make mirth ;
Have here my mittens to put on thy hands,
Other treasure have I none to present thee with.

    Mary. Now, herdsmen kind, for your coming,
To my child shall I pray
As he is heaven's king, to grant you his blessing,
And to his bliss that ye may wend at your last day.

    Then the Shepherds sing :
        Down from heaven, from heaven so high,
        Of angels there came a great company,
        With mirth and joy and great solemnity.
            They sang terly terlow
            So merrily the shepherds their pipes can blow.
                      [The Shepherds go out.

    *The scene changes.   Herod comes in and the
                   Herald.*

    Herod. I am the mightiest conqueror that ever
        walked on ground,
For I am even he that made both heaven and hell,
And of my mighty power hold up the world around.
Magog and Madroc both did I confound,
And with this bright sword their bones I broke
        asunder,
That all the wide world at those blows did wonder.
I am the cause of this great light and thunder ;
It is through my fury that such noise doth make ;
My fearful countenance the clouds so do encumber
That oftentimes for dread thereof the very earth doth
        quake.
Look ! When I with malice this bright sword do
        shake,

All the whole world, from the North to the South,
I may them destroy with one word of my mouth.
To recount unto you mine innumerable substance,
That were too much for any tongue to tell ;
For all the whole Orient is under mine obedience ;
And prince I am of purgatory and chief captain of
    hell ;
And those tyrannous traitors by force may I compel,
Mine enemies to vanquish and even to dust them drive,
And with a wink of mine eye not one to leave alive.
And therefore my herald here, called Calcas,
Warn thou every port that no ships arrive ;
Nor also any stranger through my realms pass,
But they for their passage do pay marks five.
Now speed thee forth hastily,
For they that will the contrary
Upon a gallows hanged shall be,
And, by Mahound, of me they get no grace.

    Herald. Now, lord and master, in all the haste
Thy worthy will it shall be wrought ;
And thy royal countries shall be passed
In as short time as can be thought.

                     [Exit Herald.
    Herod. Now shall our regions throughout be sought,
In every place both East and West ;
If any catiffs to me be brought,
It shall be nothing for their best.
And the while that I do rest,
Trumpets, viols, and other harmony
Shall bless the waking of my majesty.

                   [Herod goes away.

     The First King enters.

    First King. Now blessed be God, for his sweet news,
For yonder a fair bright star do I see ;
Now is he come on us among,
As the prophets said that it should be.
He said there should a babe be born

Coming of the root of Jesse,
To save mankind that was forlorn,
And truly come now is he.
Reverence and worship to him will I do,
As God and man, that all made of nought.

The Second King enters.

Second King. Out of my way I think that I am,
For tokens of this country can I none see.
Now God that on earth madest man
Send me some knowledge where that I be.
To worship that child is mine intent ;
Forth now will I take my way.
I trust some company God hath me sent,
For yonder I see a king labour on the way.
Toward him now will I ride.
Hark, comely king, I you pray,
In what land will ye thus ride,
Or whither lies your journey ?
  First King. To seek a child is mine intent,
Of whom the prophets have meant ;
The time is come ; now is he sent
By yonder star here may you see.
  Second King. I pray you with your licence,
To ride with you unto his presence ;
To him will I offer frankincense,
For the head of the whole church shall he be.

The Third King enters.

Third King. I ride wandering in ways wide,
Over mountains and dales I wot not where I am.
Now, king of all kings, send me such guide,
That I might have some knowledge of this country's
    name.
But two kings yonder I see ; to them will I ride
For to have their company, I trust they will me abide.
Hail, comely kings and noble ;
Good sirs, I pray you, whither do ye fare ?

First King. To seek a child is our intent ;
Which betokens yonder star, as ye may see.

Second King. To him I propose this present.

Third King. Sirs, I pray you, and that right humbly
With you that I may ride in company.
To almighty God now pray we,
That his precious person we may see.

They go out. Herod comes in again, and the Herald.

Herald. Hail, lord of most might,
Thy commandment is right ;
Into this land is come this night,
Three kings and with them a great company.

Herod. What do those kings in this country ?

Herald. To seek a king and a child, they say.

Herod. Of what age should he be ?

Herald. Scant twelve days old fully.

Herod. And was he so late born ?

Herald. Ay, sir, so they told me this
    same day in the morn.

Herod. Now, on pain of death, bring
    them me before.
And therefore, herald, hie thee in haste,
Ere that those kings the country have
    passed ;
Look thou bring them all three before my
    sight.
And in Jerusalem inquire more of that
    child ;
But I warn thee that thy words be mild,
For there must thou care and craft use.

Herald. Lord, I am ready at your bidding,
To serve thee as my lord and king.
For joy thereof, lo, how I spring
With light heart and fresh gambolling,
Aloft here on this mould.

A King.

Herod. Then speed thee forth hastily,
And look thou bear thee modestly.

Enter the Kings at one side ; whom the Herald
approaches.

Herald. Hail, sir kings, in your degree ;
Herod, king of these countries wide,
Desireth to speak with you all three,
And for your coming doth abide.
    First King. Sir, at his will we are prepared,
Hie us, brother, unto that lord's place
To speak with him we would be fain ;
That child that we seek, he grants us of his grace.

                   [*The Herald brings them to Herod.*

    Herald. Hail, lord without peer,
These three kings here have we brought.
    Herod. Now welcome, Sir kings, in company ;
But of my brightness, sirs, fear ye not.
Sir kings, as I understand,
A star hath guided you into my land,
Wherein great trouble you have found
By reason of its beams bright.
Wherefore, I pray you heartily,
The very truth that ye would certify
How long it is surely
Since of that star ye had first sight ?
    First King. Sir king, the very truth to say
And for to show you, as it is best,
This same is even the twelfth day
Since it appeared to us by west.
    Herod. Brother, then is there no more to say,
But with heart and will keep ye your journey ;
And come home by me, this same way,
Of your news that I might know.
You shall triumph in this country,
And with great concord banquet with me.
And that child myself then will I see,
And honour him also.
    Second King. Sir, your commandment we will fulfil,
And humbly abase ourselves thereto ;

He that wieldeth all things at will,
The right way us teach,
Sir king, that we may pass your land in peace.

   Herod. Yes, and walk softly, even at your own ease.
Your passport for a hundred days
Here shall you have of clear command ;
Our realm to travel any ways
Here shall ye have by special grant.

   Third King. Now farewell, king of high degree !
Humbly of you our leave we take.

   Herod. Then adieu, Sir kings all three,
And while I live, be bold of me ;
There is nothing in this country
But for your own ye shall it take.

               [The three Kings depart.
Now these three kings are gone on their way ;
Unwisely and unwittingly have they all wrought.
When they come again they shall die the same day,
And thus these vile wretches to death shall be brought :
Such is my liking.
He that against my laws will hold,
Be he king, or Cæsar, never so bold,
I shall them cast into cares cold,
And to death I shall them bring.

               [Then Herod goes his way.

  The three Kings come in to Mary and the Child.

   First King. Hail, lord, that all this world hath
        wrought,
Hail, God and man, together both,
For thou hast made all things of nought,
Albeit thou liest poorly here.
A cup full of gold here I have thee brought,
In tokening thou art without peer.

   Second King. Hail be thou, Lord of high magnifi-
        cence,
In tokening of priesthood and dignity of office,
To thee I offer a cup full of incense,

For it behoveth thee to have such sacrifice.

Third King. Hail be thou, lord long lookëd for,
I have brought thee myrrh for mortality,
In tokening thou shalt mankind restore
To live by thy death upon a tree.

Mary. God have mercy, kings, of your goodness ;
By the guiding of the godhead hither are ye sent ;
The provision of my sweet son, your ways who
        redress
And ghostly reward you for your present.

> *The Kings depart and on their way they say :*

First King. Sir kings, after our promise
Home by Herod I must needs go.

Second King. Now truly, brother, we can no less ;
But I am so far weary, I know not what to do.

Third King. Right so am I, wherefore I you pray,
Let us all rest us awhile upon this ground.

First King. Brother, your saying is right well unto
        my mind ;
The grace of that sweet child save us all sound.

> *The Kings lie down and sleep.   An Angel appears.*

Angel. King of Taurus, Sir Jasper ;
King of Araby, Sir Balthasar ;
Melchor, King of Aginare ;
To you now am I sent.
For dread of Herod, go you west home,
Into those parts whence ye came down.
Ye shall be buried with great renown ;
The Holy Ghost this knowledge hath sent.

> *The Angel disappears.   The Kings awake.*

First King. Awake, Sir kings, I you pray,
For the voice of an angel I heard in my dream.

Second King. That is full true that ye do say,
For he rehearsed our namës plain.

Third King. He bade that we should go down by
        west,

For dread of Herod's false betray.

First King. So for to do it is the best ;
The child that we have sought guide us the way.
Now farewell, the fairest of men so sweet,
And thanked be Jesu for his message ;
That we three together so suddenly should meet,
That dwell so wide and in strange lands ;
And here to make our presentation,
Unto this king's son cleansed so clean,
And to his mother for our salvation,
Of much mirth now may we be
That we so well have done this oblation.

Second King. Now farewell, Sir Jasper, brother to
            you,
King of Taurus, the most worthy ;
Sir Balthasar, also to you I bow,
And thank you both of your good company,
That we together have had.
He that made us to meet on hill,
I thank him now, and ever I will,
For now we may go without ill,
And of our offering be full glad.

Third King. Now since that we must needly go,
For dread of Herod, that is so wroth,
Now farewell, brother, and brother also ;
I take my leave here of you both,
This day on foot.
Now he that made us to meet on plain,
And offer to Mary and to her child,
He give us grace in heaven again
All together to meet.

*The three Kings go their ways.   Enter Herod and the
        Herald, with Knights in attendance.*

Herald. Hail king, most worthiest in might !
Hail, maintainer of courtesy through all this world wide !
Hail, the most mightiest that ever bestrode a steed !
Hail, in thine honour !

These three kings that forth were sent,
And should have come again before thee here present,
Another way, lord, home they went,
Contrary to thine honour.

    Herod. Another way !   Out, out, out !
Have those false traitors done me this deed ?
I stamp !   I stare !   I look all about !
Might I them take, I should them burn at a fire.
I rant !   I rage !   And now run I mad !
Ah !   that these villain traitors have marred this my
        plan ;
They shall be hanged if I come them to.
       [*Here Herod rages in the pageant and in the street
         also.*

Ay !   And that brat of Bethlehem he shall be dead.
How say you, Sir knights, is not this good counsel,
That all young children for this should be killed,
With sword to be slain ?
Then shall I, Herod, live in fame,
And all folk me fear and dread,
Thereto will they be full fain.

    First Knight. My lord, king Herod by name,
Thy words against my will shall be ;
To see so many young children die is shame,
Therefore counsel thereto getst thou none of me.

    Second Knight. Well said, fellow, my troth I plight ;
Sir king, perceive right well you may ;
So great a murder to see of young folk
Will make a rising in thine own country.

    Herod. A rising !   Out, out, out !

      Here Herod rages again, and says :

Out villain wretches, plague upon you I cry ;
My will utterly look that it be wrought,
Or upon a gallows both ye shall die,
By Mahound, most mightiest, that me dear hath
        bought.

    Pageant, That is, the car on which the scene was played.

First Knight. Now, cruel Herod, since we shall do
  this deed,
Your will perforce in this realm must be wrought ;
All the children of that age die they must need,
Now with all my might they shall be upsought.

Second Knight. And I will swear here, upon your
  bright sword,
All the children that I find slain shall be ;
That shall make many a mother to weep,
And be full sore afeard,
In our armour bright when they us see.

Herod. Now ye have sworn forth that ye go,
And my will that ye work both by day and night ;
And then will I for joy trip like a doe,
But when they be dead I warn you bring them before
  my sight.   [*Herod and his train go out.*

Women come in with their children.

First Woman. I lull my child wondrously sweet,
And in mine arms I do it keep,
Because that it should not cry.

Second Woman. The babe that is born in Bethlehem
  so meek,
He save my child and me from villainy.

Third Woman. Be still, be still, my little child,
The lord of lords save both thee and me ;
For Herod hath sworn, with words wild,
That all young children slain shall be.

*The Mothers then sing their children to sleep with
  this song.*

Lulla, lullay, ye little tiny child ;
  By-by, lulla, lullay, ye little tiny child,
    By-by, lulla, lullay.

Oh sisters two, how may we do,
  For to preserve this day,
This poor youngling ? for whom we do sing
  By-by, lulla, lullay.

Herod the king, in his raging,
Charged he hath this day,
His men of might, in his own sight,
All young children to slay.

Then woe is me, poor child, for thee
And ever mourn I may :
For thy parting, neither say nor sing
By-by, lulla, lullay.

Herod's Knights enter.

First Knight. See ye, old wives, whither are ye
away ?
What ye bear in your arms needs must we see.
If they be men children, die they must this day,
For at Herod's will all things must be.
Second Knight. And I in hands once them seize ;
Them for to slay nought will I spare.
We must fulfil Herod's commandment,
Else we be as traitors and cast in all care.
First Woman. Sir knights, of your courtesy,
This day shame not your chivalry,
But on my child have pity,
For my sake in this place.
Second Woman. He that slays my child in sight,
If that my strokes on him may light,
Be he squire or knight,
I hold him but lost !
Third Woman. Sits he never so high in saddle,
But I shall make his brains addle,
And here with my pot ladle,
With him will I fight !
I shall lay on him, as though I mad were,
With this same womanly gear,
Whether that he be king or knight.
                    [*Here the Knights slay the children.*
First Knight. Who heard ever such a cry ?
Of women, that their children have lost,

And greatly rebuking chivalry,
Throughout this realm in every coast,
Which many a man's life is like to cost.
For this great wrong that here is done,
I fear much vengeance thereof will come.

    Second Knight. Ay, brother, such tales may we not
        tell,
Wherefore to the king let us go ;
For he is like to bear the peril,
Which was the cause that we did so.
Yet must they all be brought him to,
With wains and wagons fully freight ;
I trow there will be a sorry sight.

                          [They come to Herod.

    First Knight. Lo, Herod king, here mayst thou see,
How many thousands we have slain.
    Second Knight. And needs thy will fulfilled must be,
But may no man attempt this again.

Enter the Herald.

    Herald. Herod king, I shall thee tell,
All thy deeds are come to nought ;
This child is gone in Egypt to dwell ;
Lo, sire, in thine own land what wonders be wrought.
    Herod. Into Egypt ! alas for woe !
Longer in land here I cannot abide ;
Saddle my palfrey, for in haste must I go ;
After yon traitors now will I ride
Them for to slay !
Now all men I send fast
Into Egypt in haste,
All that country will I cross
Till I may come them to !

The end of the play of the Taylors and Shearmen

CHAPTER XII.—THE CHESTER SHEPHERDS' PLAY

A MORE elaborate version of the coming of the shepherds to Bethlehem is the Shepherds' Play of Chester. Here the three shepherds come in and talk about their flocks, and then fall to a hearty meal.   Then comes a wrestling bout, which thus introduces on to the stage one of the oldest of British sports.   This shows that the play is no longer a churchman's play, but a play of the people ; a wrestling bout could scarcely have taken place in the church.   Afterwards the angels appear to the shepherds, leaving them to make clumsy guesses at the meaning of the Latin hymn sung by the heavenly host.   Finally they come to Bethlehem, where, like the shepherds of Coventry, they make simple homely presents to the new born Babe, and resolve to serve him all their days.

The Play of the Shepherds

(The Painters and Glaziers' Play of Chester)

Enter First Shepherd.

First Shepherd. On wolds I have walked full wild,
Under bushes my bower to build,
From stiff storms my sheep to shield,
My seemly wethers to save ;
From comely Conway unto Clyde,
Under tents them to hide,
A better shepherd on no side
No earthly man may have.
For with walking wearied I have, methought,
Beside the which my sheep I sought ;
My taleful rams are in my thought

Taleful, To the full number.

Them to save and heal.
From the shrewd scab it sought,
Or the rot, if it were wrought,
If the cough had them caught,
Of it I could them heal.
Lo, here be my herbs safe and sound,
Wisely wrought for every wound ;
They would a whole man bring to ground
Within little while ;
But no fellowship here have I,
Save myself alone in good fay ;
Therefore after one fast will I cry,
But first will I drink, if I may.   *[He drinks.*
Ho ! Harvey, ho !
Drive thy sheep to the low ;
Thou may not hear, except I blow
As ever have I heal.
    [He blows his horn, enter Second Shepherd.
   Second Shepherd. It is no shame for to show
How I was set to sow,
With the feather of a crow,
A clout upon my heel.   *[They sit down.*
Fellow, now we be well met,
Although methinks it needs
Had we Tudde here by us set,
There might we sit and feed us.
   First Shepherd. Yea, to feed us friendly in fay,
How might we have our service ay,
Ay thou must low, by this day,
Tudde is deaf and may not well hear us.
   Second Shepherd. Ho ! Tudde, come for thy
      fatherkin !   *[He shouts, but in a subdued voice.*
   First Shepherd. Nay, fay, thy voice is wondrous
      dim ;
Why, knowest thou not him ?
Fie, man, for shame !

Heal, Salvation.

Call him " Tudde, Tibb's son,"
And then will the shrew come,
For, in good faith, it is his wont
To love well his dam's name.
    Second Shepherd. Ho ! Tudde, Tibb's son !

Enter Third Shepherd.

    Third Shepherd. Sir, in faith now I come,
For yet have I not all done
That I have to do ;
To seeth salve for our sheep ;
And lest my wife should it wit
With great gravel and grit
I scour an old pan.
Ashamed am I not to show
No point belonging to my craft,
No better, that I well know,
In land is nowhere left.
For to good men this is not unknown,
To husbands that be hereabouts,
That each man must to his wife bow,
And commonly for fear of a clout.
All is for fear of our dame Kenye,
Now will I cast my ware here by,
And hie fast that I were at Hankin.
Hankin, hold up thy hand and have me,
That I were on height there by thee.
             [Hankin helps him up to a seat.
    Second Shepherd.. Now seeing God hath gathered us
        together,
With good heart I thank him of his grace.
Welcome be thou, well fair weather,
Tudd, will we shape us to some solace.
    Third Shepherd. Solace would best be seen
That we shape us to our supper ;
For meat and drink well, I ween,
To each man is most dear.
    First Shepherd. Lay forth, each man, each one,

What he hath left of his livery ;
And I will put forth my pinch,
With my part, first of us all three.

    Second Shepherd. And such store as my wife had,
In your sight soon shall you see,
At our beginning us for to glad,
For in good meat there is much glee.
Here is bread this day was baken ;
Onions, garlics, and leeks,
Butter that bought was in Blackon,
And green cheese that will grease your cheeks.

    Third Shepherd. And here ale of Halton I have,
And what meat I had to my hire ;
A pudding may no man deprave,
And a jannock of Lancashire.
Lo, here a sheep's head soused in ale,
And a grain to lay on the green,
And sour milk my wife hath made,
A noble supper as is well seen.

    First Shepherd. Now will I cast off my cloak,
And put out part of my livery,
And put out that I have in my poke,
And a pig's foot from pudding pury.

    Third Shepherd. Abide, fellows, and you shall see
        here
The hot meat servëd here,
Gammons and other good meat in faith,
A pudding with a prick in the end.

    First Shepherd. My satchel to take out
To shepherd am I not ashamed ;
And this tongue pared round about,
With my tongue it shall be tamed.

                    [Then they eat together.
Housing enough have we here,
While that we have heaven over our heads :

    Livery, Day's food.   **Jannock**, An oatcake.
    Pudding pury, Porridge.
    Tamed, Tasted ; see also four lines farther on.

Now to wet our mouths time were,
This flagon will I tame, if thou rede us.

 Third Shepherd. And of this bottle now will I bib,
For here is but of the best ;
Such liquor makes me to live,
This game may nowhere be left.

 First Shepherd. Fellows, now our belly be full,
Think we on him that keeps our flocks.
Blow thy horn and call after Trull,
And keep him some of our bytlockes !

 Second Shepherd. Well said, Hankin, by my sooth,
For that shrew I suppose seeks us.
My horn to blow I will not let
Till that lad have some of our leeks.

 Third Shepherd. Leeks to his livery is liking,
Such a lad nowhere in land is.
Blow a note for that nithing,
While that horn now in thy hand is.

 First Shepherd. With this horn I shall make a
   " howe "
That he and all heaven shall hear ;
Yonder lad, that sits on a low,
The noise of this horn shall hear.

    [*Then he shall blow, and Trull shall come in.*
Trull, take heed to my talking,
For thy teeth here is good tugging,
While thy wethers be walking,
And on this loin thou may have good lugging.

 Trull. Fie on your loins and on your livery !
Your livery, livers and tongues !
Your sauce, your food, your savoury,
Your sitting without any songs.

 Second Shepherd. For thou saves our sheep,
Good knave, take keep ;
See thou may not sleep,
Come eat of this sauce.

    Bytlockes, Morsels of food.

Trull. Nay, the dirt is so deep
And the grubs thereon do creep
At home, at thy house.
Therefore meat, if I may,
Of your dighting to-day
Will I nought, by no way,
Till I have my wages.
  Third Shepherd. Trull,
        boy, for God's fee !
Come eat a morsel with me,
And then wrestle will we
Here on this green.
  Trull. That shall I never
        flee,
Though it be with all three,
To lay my livery,
That wages will I hold.
  [*Then he goes up to his
        masters.*
Now comes Trull the true,
A turn to take have I tight
With my masters, or I rue,
Put him forth that is most of might.
  First Shepherd. Trull, better never thou knew,
Eat of this meat for a knight.
  Trull. Nay, spare I will, though I spue,
All upon thy head shall light.
  Second Shepherd. How should we suffer all this shame,
Of a shrew thus to be shent ?
  Third Shepherd. This lad lusts to be lamed
And lose a limb ere he went.
  Trull. Have done, begin we this game ;
That were little dole to your dame
If in midst Dee thou wert drent.
  First Shepherd. False lad, fie on thy face,
On this ground thou shalt have a fall.

Trull.

(The shepherds would be similarly
clothed, but should be older men.)

Shent, Abused, cursed.

Hence one, and hold that thou haste,
If thou hap have, all go to all.

   Trull. And these sires here to solace,
Hankin, shepherd, shame thee I shall ;
Worth thou art worse than thou was,
Ware lest thou fall here by the wall.

[Then he throws the First Shepherd.

   Second Shepherd. Boy, lest I break thy bones,
Kneel down and ask me a boon,
Lest I destroy thee here on these stones :
Cease, lest I shame thee too soon.

   Trull. Glow thee to grins and groans,
Good were thee thy old rages to save sound ;
Little doubt of such drones,
Leither tyke, for thy deeds are done.

[Then he throws the Second Shepherd.

   Third Shepherd. Out, alas ! he lies on his loins,
But let me go now to that lad !

   Trull. Both your back here to me bend ;
For all your boast I hold you full bad ;
Hold your backs and your hinder loins,
Then hope I to have as I to-fore had.

[Then he throws the Third Shepherd.

Lie there, leither, in the lake,
My livery now will I take ;
This curry, this clout, and this cake,
For ye be cast, now will I catch.
On this wold with this I will walk,
All the world wonder on the watch !

[Then he goes away.

   First Shepherd. Fellows, this a foul case is,
That we be thus cast out by a knave ;
All against our will he has his,
But I must needs hold the harm that I have.

   Second Shepherd. That I have, needs must I hold,
Of these unhappy harms oft hear I :

    Leither tyke, Wicked dog.

Therefore will I wait on this wold
Upon the weather, for I am weary.

Third Shepherd. Though we be weary, no wonder,
What between wrestling and walking !
Oft we may be in thought, we be now under,
God amend it with his making !

[*Then they shall sit down and the star shall appear.*

First Shepherd. What is all this light here,
That shines so bright here,
On my black beard ?
For to see this light here,
A man might be affright here,
For I am afeard.

Second Shepherd. Afraid for a fray now
May we all be now ;
Ah ! yet it is night,
Yet seemeth it day now.
See I such a sight !

Third Shepherd. Such a light seeming,
And a light gleaming,
Lets me to look ;
All to my deeming,
From a star streaming
It to me stroke.

Trull [*coming in again*]. That star, if it stand,
To see will I find,
Though might light fail ;
While I may live on land,
Why should I find,
If it will avail ?

[*Then looking up at the firmament he says :*
Ah ! God mighty is,
As yonder starlight is,
Of the sun this sight is,
As it now shines.

First Shepherd. It seems as I now see

Lets, Hinders.

A bright star to be,
There to abide.
From it we may not flee,
Till it down glide.

    Second Shepherd. Fellows, will we
Kneel down on our knee,
After comfort.   [*They kneel.*

    Trull. Lord of this light
Guide us some sight,
Why that it is sent.
Before this night,
Was I never so affright
Of the firmament.

Then an Angel sings :

Gloria in excelsis Deo
Et in terra pax hominibus
Bonæ voluntatis.

    First Shepherd. Fellows in fear,
May you not hear
This singing on high ?

    Second Shepherd. On " glore " and in " glere,"
Yet no man was near
Within our sight.

    First Shepherd. As I then deemed,
" Scellsis " it seemed
That he sang.

    Third Shepherd. What song was this, say ye,
That they sang to us all three ?
Expounded shall it be
Ere we hence pass,
For I am eldest of degree,
And also best, as seemeth me :
It was " glore, glare," with a glee,
It was neither more nor less.

    Trull. Nay, it was " glory, glory, glorious ! "

Gloria, etc., " Glory to God in the highest, and on earth peace to
    men of good will."

Methought that note ran over the house :
A seemly man he was, and curious,
But soon away he was.

    First Shepherd. Nay it was " glory, glory," with a
        glow !
And much of " cellsis " was thereto :
As ever I have rest or rue,
Much he spoke of " glasse."

    Second Shepherd. Nay it was neither glasse nor
        glee ;
Therefore, fellow, now stand by.

    Third Shepherd. By my faith, he was some spy,
Our sheep for to steal ;
Or else he was a man of our craft,
For seemly he was and wondrous daft.

    Second Shepherd. Nay, by God ! it was a " gloria,"
Said Gabriel when he began so ;
He had a much better voice than I have,
As in heaven all others have so.

    Third Shepherd. Will ye hear how he sang " selsis " ?
For on that sadly he set him,
Neither sings " sir," nor well " sis,"
Nor " pax, merry Maud, when she so met him."

    First Shepherd. Now pray we to him with good
        intent,
And sing I will and me embrace,
That he will let us to be hent,
And to send us of his grace.

    Trull. Sing we now, let us see,
Some song will I assay :
All men now sing after me,
For music of me learn you may.

    Then they shall sing : " Trolly, lolly ; trolly, low."

    Third Shepherd. Now wend we forth to Bethlehem,
That is best our song to be.

    First Shepherd. Now follow we the star that shineth,
Till we come to that holy stable ;

To Bethlehem bend our limbs,
Follow we it without any fable.

Second Shepherd. Follow we it and hie full fast,
Such a friend loth us to fail ;
Launch on, I will not be the last,
Upon Mary for to marvel.

                [Here they journey toward Bethlehem.

    Third Shepherd. Stint now, go no more steps,
For now the star beginneth to stand ;
Here by ; that good be our haps
We see by, our saviour found.

       Here the Angel appears to them and says :

Shepherds, of this sight
Be ye not affright,
For this is God's might,
Take this in mind :
To Bethlehem now right,
There you shall see in sight,
That Christ is born to-night,
To save all mankind.

    Trull. To Bethlehem take we the way,
For with you I think to wend,
That prince of peace for to pray,
Heaven to have at our end.
And sing we all, I rede,
Some mirth to his majesty ;
For certain now show it in deed,
The king's son of heaven is he.

        [Here they come to the stable where the child is.

    First Shepherd. Sim, Sim, verily
Here I see Mary,
And Jesus Christ fast by,
Wrapped in hay.

    Second Shepherd. Kneel we down in hie,
And pray we him of mercy,
And welcome him worthily,
That woe does away.

Third Shepherd. Away all our woe is,
And many man's mo is!
Christ Lord, let us kiss
Thy cradle or thy clothes.

Trull. Solace now, to see this
Builds in my breast bliss,
Never after to do amiss
Things that him loath is.

First Shepherd. Whatever this old man that here
    is,
Take heed how his head is hoar,
His beard is like a bush of briars,
With a pound of hair about his mouth and more.

Third Shepherd. Why, with his beard, though it
    hides,
Right well to her he heeds.

Mary. Shepherds, soothly I see
That my son you hither sent,
Through God's might in majesty,
That in me light, and here is lent.

Joseph. Good men, go! preach forth this thing,
All together and not in twain,
That you have seen your heavenly king
Come, and all mankind to win.

First Shepherd. Great God, sitting on thy throne,
That made all things of nought,
Now we may thank thee, each one,
This is he that we have sought.

Second Shepherd. Go we near anon,
With such as we have brought,
Ring, brooch, or precious stone,
Let us see if we have ought to proffer.

Third Shepherd. Let us do him homage.

First Shepherd. Who shall go first? the page?

Second Shepherd. Nay, ye be father of age,
Therefore ye must offer.

In twain, Separate.

First Shepherd. Hail, king of heaven so high !
Born in a crib,
Mankind unto thee
Thou hast made fully.
Hail, child ! born in a maiden's bower,
Prophets did tell thou shouldst be our succour,
Thus clerks do say.
Lo, I bring thee a bell :
I pray thee save me from hell,
So that I may with thee dwell,
    And serve thee for ay.
    Second Shepherd. Hail thee, emperor
      of hell
    And of heaven also !
    The fiend shalt thou fell,
    That ever hath been false.
    Hail thee, maker of the star,
    That stood us before ;
    Hail thee, blessedful bairn,
    Lo, son, I bring thee a flacket,
    Thereby hangs a spoon,
    To eat thy pottage withal at noon,
    As I myself full ofttimes have done,
    With heart I pray thee to take.
    Third Shepherd. Hail, prince without

The Virgin and
Child.

      any peer,
    That mankind shall relieve !
Hail thee, foe unto Lucifer,
The which beguilèd Eve !
Hail thee, granter of hap,
For in earth now thou dwellest.
Lo, son, I bring thee a cape,
For I have nothing else :
This gift, son, I bring thee is but small,
And though I come the hindmost of all,
When thou shalt them to thy bliss call,
    Good Lord, yet think on me.
  Trull. My dear, with duty unto thee I me dress,

My state and fellowship that I do not lose,
For to save me from all ill sickness,
I offer unto thee a pair of my wife's old hose ;
For other gifts, my son,
Have I none for to give,
That is worth anything at all,
But my good heart, while I live,
And my prayers till death do me call.

First Shepherd. Now farewell, mother and maid,
And that we may from sin fall,
And stand ever in thy grace,
Our Lord God be with thee.

Second Shepherd. Brethren, let us all three
Singing walk homewards ;
Unkind will I in no case be,
But preach ever that I can, and cry,
As Gabriel taught by his grace me,
Springing away hence will I.

Third Shepherd. Over the sea, and I may have grace,
I will wend and about go now,
To preach this in every place,
And sheep will I keep none now.

Trull. I rede we us agree
For our misdeeds amends to make ;
For so now I will
And to that child wholly me betake ;
For ever verily
Shepherd's craft here I forsake,
And to an anchorage hereby
I will in my prayers watch and wake.

First Shepherd. And I am here meek
To praise God to pay,
To walk by stile and street,
In wildness to walk ever ;
And I will no man meet,

Anchorage, The dwelling of an anchorite or hermit.

But for my living I shall them pray,
Barefoot on my feet,
And thus will I live ever and ay.
For ay ever once,
This world I full refuse,
My miss to amend with moans.
Turn to thy fellows and kiss,
I yield, for in youth
We have been fellows, i-wis ;
Therefore lend us your mouth,
And friendly let us kiss.

    Second Shepherd. From London to Louth
Such another shepherd I not were ;
Both strangers and friends
God grant you amen.

    Third Shepherd. To that bliss bring you,
Great God, if thy will be ;
Amen, all sing you :
Goodmen, farewell.

    Trull. Well for to fare each friend,
God of his might grant you ;
For here now we make an end,
Farewell, for we go from you now.

CHAPTER XIII.—THE MASSACRE
OF THE INNOCENTS *Mathew 2*

CHESTER also produced a most interesting version of
the story of the *Slaughter of the Innocents*. In the
great days of adventure and chivalry, when the Black
Prince and his knights were winning glory at Crécy
and Poictiers, it became usual for books to be com-
piled of stories of valiant knights, who went about
rescuing damsels and slaying dragons, and generally
speaking behaving in a highly romantic way, quite
different from the actual grim realities of warfare in
France. It was not long before people began to see

the ridiculous side of these stories, and the most famous burlesque of them was Cervantes' humorous adventures of the ridiculous hero, Don Quixote de la Mancha. Naturally the reading of tales of chivalry was the amusement of the upper class, for they alone had the ability to read or the money to buy books, but the citizens knew these stories well, and they too saw their ridiculous side. We find the gildsmen of Chester obtaining their burlesque of knights-errant, not by writing a new book or play, but by doctoring up their already existing story of *Herod's Slaughter of the Children*, and making him send out his knights to slay a few innocent babes, as though he were some great king sending out his heroes on chivalrous adventure.

The Slaughter of the Innocents

(The Goldsmiths and Masons' Play of Chester)

Herod. Princes, prelates of price,
Barons in balmer and biss,
Beware of me all that be wise,
That wield I all my will !
Say no man anything is his,
But only at my devise ;
For all this world lies
To spare and eke to spill.
My subjects all that here be set,
Baron, burgess, and baronet,
Be bound to me, or you I beat,
And at my bidding be.
And these false traitors that me behight
To have come again on this same night,
But another way have taken their flight,
This way durst they not take.
Therefore that boy, by God almight

Balmer and biss, Names of precious stuffs.

Shall be slain soon in your sight,
And, though it be against the right,
A thousand for his sake.
Alas! what purpose had that page,
That is so young and tender of age,
That would bereave my heritage,
That am so mild of might?
But since it may none other be,
But these kings are gone from me,
I think to put him down;
Because I know not which is he,
All for his sake shall be slay.
Ho! Pretty Pratte, my messenger!
Come hither to me withouten were,
For thou must go full hastily
Into Judye this day,
After my doughty and comely knights,
And bid them hie with all their mights,
And they let for no fights,
Bring them all without delay.

Herald. Yes, my lord of high renown,
To do your bidding I am bound.

Herod. Now mighty Mahound be with thee!
And ever to be in fear!

[*The Herald goes out, and soon returns, bringing the
      Knights with him.*

Herald. Hail, comely king, sitting in see,
Here be these knights come to thee,
They be men of great degree,
To hear of your talent.

First Knight. Hail, comely king! crowned in gold,
Each king and Cæsar bends at your beck,
If any were that with your grace fight would,
Such strokes for your sake sore shall be set.

Herod. Welcome, our knights, that be so gente,
Now will we tell you our intent,

Withouten were, Without doubt.

What is this cause we for you sent
So soon and hastily.
Yesterday to this city,
When we were in our royalty,
There came to us kings three,
And told us their intent ;
To see a child that born should be,
That was said by prophecy,
That should be king of Judye,
And of many another land.
We gave them leave to search and see,
And come again to this city,
And if he were of such degree,
We would not him withstand ;
But and they had come here again
All three traitors should have been
    slain,
And also that wicked swain,
And all for his sake.
Out, alas ! what may this be ?
For I know not which is he,
Therefore all knaves children in
    this city
On them should fall the wrack ;
For we know not that child well,
And we therefore should go to
    hell ;
All the children of Israel
We deem them to be slain.
But yet I burn as doth the fire,
What for wrath, what for ire,
Till this be brought to end.
Therefore, my knights good and keen,
Have done ; be live ; go ; wreck my teen !
Go slay that shrew, let it be seen
That you be men of might.

A Knight.

Knaves children, Boy babies.   *Teen*, Vexation.

You must hie you out of this town
To Bethlehem, as fast as you may,
All knaves children, by my crown,
You must slay this night.
   First Knight. Alas ! lord and king of bliss,
Send you after us for this ?
A villainy it were, i-wis,
For my fellow and me.
   Second Knight. My lief lord of great renown,
We shall wreck us as we may,
Whether he be king, or champion,
Stiffer than ever Samson was,
Surely I shall drive them down ;
But for to kill such a counjon,
Me shames sore, by Mahound !
To go in any place.
   Herod. Nay, it is neither one nor two
That ye shall slay, as must I go,
But a thousand and yet mo,
Take this in your mind ;
Because I know not which that shrew is,
Therefore, lest you of him miss,
You must slay forsooth, i-wis,
All that you may find,
All knaves children within two years
And one day old.
   First Knight. It shall be done, lord, in hie,
Shall none be left witterly,
We shall go search by and by
In Bethlehem all about ;
To Bethlehem that borough I am bound,
With this spear I think to assay
To kill many a small counjon ;
And stoutly with strokes them destroy,
Shall never one escape by my will,
Of two years age and less.

Counjon, Fellow.

Second Knight. Therefore to me take good keep,
My name is Sir Lancler bold.
They that me teen I lay to sleep
On every side ;
Through Bethlehem I will spring,
For I must now at your bidding,
Right all down shall I ding
These lads every one.

    First Knight. Farewell, my lord, and have good
          day,
For hardly I dare this say,
Not for no boast, in good fay,
It is not my manner ;
I would I might find in my way,
Samson in his best array,
To see whether I durst afray,
To fight with him right here.

    Herod. Nay, I know well, or thou swear,
That thou art a doughty man of war,
And though Samson were here,
Soon he should be slain.
But speed you fast, for my prayer,
And hie you fast again.   *[They go away.*

*The scene changes. Women come in with their children.
        The Knights appear.*

    First Knight. Haste down, fellow, haste down fast,
That these queans were down cast,
And their children in haste,
And kill them all with clouts.

    Second Knight. Yea, sirs, we dwell all too long,
Therefore go we them among ;
They hope to have come wrong
That go so fast away.

    First Woman. Whom callest thou quean, scabbed
        bitch ?

              Teen, Vex, injure.

Second Woman. Be thou so hardy, I thee warn
To handle my son that is so sweet,
This distaff on thy head shall meet,
Ere we hence go.

    Second Knight. Dame, thy son, in good fay,
He must of me learn a play,
He must hop, ere I go away,
Upon my spear end.

    First Woman. Out and out ! and welaway !
That ever I did abide this day ;
One stroke I will assay
To give, ere that I wend.

    Second Woman. Out !   Out on this thief !
My love, my lord, my life, my life !
Did never man nor woman grieve,
To suffer such torment ;
But yet avenged will I be :—
Have here one, two, or three !

                      [She beats him with her distaff.
Bear the king this from me,
And that I it him send.

    First Knight. Come hither to me, dame Purnell,
And show me here thy son snell :
For the king hath bidden me quell
All that we find may.

    First Woman. My son ! nay, strong thief,
For as I have good proof,
Thou do my child any grief,
I shall crack thy crown.

                  [Then the Knight kills the first child.
Out. out ! and woe is me !
Thief, thou shalt be hanged high !
My child is dead now I see,
My sorrow may not cease.
Thou shalt be hanged on a tree,
And all thy fellows with thee,

            Snell, Quickly.

All the men in this country
Shall not make thee peace.

          [Then the Second Knight kills another child.

  Second Woman. Out, out, out, out !
You shall be hanged, the rout,
Though be ye never so stout !
Full foul ye have done.
This child was brought to me
To look to, thieves ; who be ye ?
He was not mine, as you may see,
He was the king's son.
I shall tell, while I may drye,
His child was slain before my eye.
Thieves, you shall be hanged high,
May I come to his hall.
But, ere I go, have thou one !
And thou another, Sir John !
For to the king I will anon,
To plaint upon you all.

    [Then they go to Herod, who is feasting and making
        merry.

  Second Woman. Lo, lord, look and see
The child that thou sent to me,
Men of thine own maynee
Have slain it, here they be.
  Herod. Fie, woman, fie ! God give thee pain,
Why did thou say that child was not mine ?
But it is vengeance, as drink I wine,
And that is now well seen.
  Second Woman. Yes, lord, they see well aright
Thy son was like to have been a knight,
For in good harness he was dight,
Painted wondrous gay ;
Yet was I never so sore affright,

Drye, Suffer.   *Maynee*, Household.

When the spears were through him thrust,
Lord, so little was my might,
When they began to fray.

    Herod. He was right surely in silk array,
In gold and pearl that was so gay,
They might well know by his array,
He was a king's son;
What the devil is this to say!
Why were thy wits so away?
Could thou not speak, could thou not pray,
And say it was my son?
Alas! what the devil is this to moan?
Alas! my days be now done;
I wot I must die soon:
Bootless is me to make moan,
For damnëd I must be;
My legs rot and my arms,
That now I see of fiends swarms,
I have done so many harms,
From hell coming after me;
I have done so much woe,
And never good, since I might go,
Therefore I see coming my foe,
To fetch me to hell.
I bequeath here in this place
My soul to be with Sathanas.
I die now, alas! alas!
I may no longer dwell.

   Then he makes signs as of a dying man, and
the Demon shall come.

    Demon. Ware, ware! for now unwarly walks your
       woe,
For I am swifter than was the doe,
I am come to fetch this lord you fro,
In woe evermore to dwell;
And with this crooked cammock your backs I shall cloe,

     Cammock, A crooked stick.

And all false believers I burn and blow,
That from the crown of the head to the toe
I leave no right whole fell.
From Lucifer, that lord, hither I am sent,
To fetch this king's soul here present,
Into hell to bring him there to be lent,

Hell mouth.

Ever to live in woe.
There fire burns, blow and brent,
In there shall be this lord verament,
His place therein evermore is hent,
His body never to go fro.—
No more shall you trespass, by my leauté,
That fill your measures falsely,

Leauté, Loyalty.

Shall bear this lord company,
They get no other grace ;
I will you bring thus into woe,
And come again and fetch mo,
As fast as I may go,
Farewell and have good day.

   [*Here Herod dies, and the Demon carries him off.*

CHAPTER XIV.—THE WAKEFIELD SALUTATION *Luke 1: 26-28*

BESIDES the comic characters of Noah's Wife, Herod, and even Judas Iscariot and the Devil, the mystery plays also reproduced a good deal of the ordinary everyday life of the people.   In the play of Wakefield, in Yorkshire, the meeting between the Virgin Mary and Elizabeth is a very human and natural scene between two women, who inquire after common acquaintances and rejoice over each other's good fortune.   The scene is quite short; but besides the talk between the two women, it contains a paraphrase of the *Magnificat*, the hymn traditionally associated with the Virgin Mary, which here, as in the gospel, comes as the very natural prayer of thanks from a woman who has just realized the full importance of her choice as the Mother of our Lord.

Here Beginneth the Salutation of Elizabeth

Enter Mary and Elizabeth, meeting.

Mary. My lord of Heaven, that sits on high,
And all things sees with his eye,
   Thee save, Elizabeth.
Elizabeth. Welcome, Mary, blessed bloom,
Joyful am I at thy come

Come, Coming.

To me, from Nazareth.
Mary. How stands it with you, dame, of quiet ?
Elizabeth. Well, my daughter and dear heart,
    As can for mine age.
Full long shall I the better be,
That I may speak my fill with thee,
    My dear kinswoman ;
To wit how thy friendës fare,
In thy country where they are,
    Thereof tell me thou can,
And how thou farest, my dear darling.
    Mary. Well, dame, grammercy your asking
    For good, I wot, ye ask.
    Elizabeth. And Joachim, thy father, at home,
And Anna, my niece, and thy dame,
    How stands it with him and her ?
    Mary. Dame, yet are they both alive,
Both Joachim and Anna his wife.
    Elizabeth. Else were my heart full sore.
    Mary. Dame, God that all things may,
Yield you that you say
    And bless you therefore.
    Elizabeth. And this time may I bless,
When my Lord's mother is
    Come thus unto me.
For since that time full well I wot,
The sound of angel voice it smote,
    And rang now in mine ear.
And also, Mary, blest be thou,
That steadfastly would trow
    The words of our heavenly king.
Therefore all things shall now be known,
That unto thee were said or sent,
    By the angel greeting.
    Mary. Magnificat anima mea Dominum ;
My soul loves my lord above,

Magnificat, etc., " My soul doth magnify the Lord."
(2,753)

9

My spirit glads with love,
     In God that is my saviour.
Lo, whereof what me shall betide—
All nations of every side
     Blessed shall me call ;
For he that is full of might
Mighty things to me has dight ;
     His name be blessed over all.
And his mercy is also,
From kind to king to all those
     That are him dreading ;
Might in his arms be wrought,
And destroyed in his thought
     Proud men and high bearing.
Mighty men from their seat he sped,
And he heightened in their stead
     The meek men of heart ;
The hungry with all good he filled
And left the rich downcast
     Them to unquiet.
Israel has under law,
His own son has in awe,
     By means of his mercy ;
As he told before by name,
To our father, Abraham,
     And said of his body.
Elizabeth, mine aunt dear,
My leave I take of you here,
     For I dwell now full long.
     Elizabeth. Wilt thou now go, God's fere ?
Come, kiss me, daughter, with good cheer,
     Ere thou hence go.
Farewell now, thou noble child,
I pray thee, be of comfort good,
     For thou art full of grace.
Greet well all our kin of blood ;

Fere, Companion.

That Lord, that thee with grace imbued,
    He save all in this place.

[*Here endeth the Salutation of Elizabeth.*]

John 11: 1-45

CHAPTER XV.—THE RAISING OF LAZARUS

ANOTHER of the more serious and dignified of the
mystery plays was that which presented the miracle
of the raising of Lazarus, as it was performed at Wakefield. This play is serious throughout, and it concludes with a sermon from the risen Lazarus to his
audience on the vanity of human pomp and riches.
This idea of the levelling power of death, to whom
great and small alike must bow, has been a common
theme in all ages, but it seems to have had a peculiar
fascination for the people of the fifteenth century.

Here Beginneth the Lazarus

Enter Jesus and his Disciples.

Jesus. Come now, brethren, and go with me,
We will pass forth into Judye,
To Bethany will we wend
To visit Lazarus that is our friend.
Gladly I would we with him speak,
I tell you truly he is sick.

    Peter. I rede not that ye thither go,
The Jews hold you for their foe ;
I rede ye come not in that stede,
For if ye do, then be ye dead.

    John. Master, trust thou not the Jew ;
For many a day since thou them knew,
And last time that we were there
We thought to have been dead therefore.

    Thomas. When we were last in that country

Rede, Advise, counsel.

The other day, both thou and we,
We thought that thou there should be slain ;
Wilt thou now go thither again ?

Jesus. Hearken, brother, my words heed,
Lazarus our friend is fallen asleep ;
The way to him now will we take,
To stir that knight, and to him wake.

Peter. Sir, methinks it were the best
To let him sleep and take his rest ;
And see that no man come him near,
For if he sleep then may he mend.

Jesus. I say to you that without fail,
No careful watch may him avail,
And sleep can stand him in no stead ;
I tell you truly he is dead ;
Therefore I say you now at last
Cease this speech, and go we fast.

Thomas. Sir, whatsoever ye bid us do
We assent us well thereto ;
I hope to God ye shall not find
One of us shall lag behind ;
For any peril that befall
Wend we with our master all.

As they approach Lazarus's tomb, Martha enters.

Martha. Help me, Lord, and give me rede,
Lazarus my brother now is dead,
That was to thee both loved and dear ;
He had not died had thou been here.

Jesus. Martha, Martha, thou may be fain,
Thy brother shall rise and live again.

Martha. Lord, I wot that he shall rise
And come before the good justice ;
For at the dreadful day of doom
Then may ye keep him when he come.

Jesus. I warn you, both man and wife,
That I am rising, I am life ;
And whoso truly trusts on me,

That I was ever and ay shall be,
One thing I shall him give,
Though he be dead, yet shall he live.
Say, woman, trust thou this?

Martha. Yea, forsooth, my lord of bliss,
Else were I greatly to mispraise,
For all is truthful that thou says.

Jesus. Go tell thy sister Magdalene,
That I come he may be fain.

Martha fetches her sister Mary, saying :

Sister, leave this sorrowful band,
Our lord comes here at hand,
And his apostles with him also.

Mary. Ah, for God's love let me go ;
[*To Jesus.*] Blessed be he that send me grace,
That I may see thee in this place.
Lord, much sorrow may men see
Of my sister here, and me.
We are heavy as any lead
For our brother that thus is dead.
Had thou been here and him seen,
Dead, forsooth, had he not been.

Jesus. Hither to you, come we are
To bring you comfort from your care,
But see no faintness nor no sloth
Bring you out of steadfast truth,
Then shall I do what I have said.
Lo, where have ye his body laid ?

Mary. Lord, if it be thy will,
I fear by this he savours ill ;
For it is now the fourth day gone
Since he was laid 'neath yonder stone.

Jesus. I told thee right as there thou stood
That thy truth should ay be good ;
And if thou may that fulfil,
All be done right at thy will.

[*Here Jesus weeps, saying :*

Father, I pray thee that thou raise,
Lazarus that was thy servant,
And bring him out of his misease
And out of hell pain.
When I thee pray thou says always
My will is such as thine ;
Therefore will we now eke his days,
To me thou wilt incline.
Come forth, Lazarus, stand us by
In earth shalt thou no longer lie ;

[*Lazarus comes from the tomb, in his graveclothes.*

Take and loose him foot and hand,
And from his throat take the band,
And the sudary take him fro,
And all that gear, and let him go.

Lazarus. Lord, that all things made of nought,
Loving be to thee,
That such wonder here has wrought,
Greater may none be.
When I was dead to hell I sought,
And thou, through thy great power,
Raised me up, and thence me brought
Behold and ye may see.
There is none so firm in place,
Nor none so proud in might,
Nor none so doughty in his deed,
Nor none so high on throne,
No king, no knight, no wight in weed,
From death hath made him safe.
On flesh he was wont to feed,
He shall be worms' food.
On your mirror here ye look,
And let me be your book,
    Your sample take by me ;
Each one in such array with death they shall be dight,
And closèd cold in clay, whether he be king or knight ;

Sudary, Napkin.   *Wight in weed*, Man in clothing.

For all his garments gay, that seemly were in sight,
His flesh shall fret away, with many a woeful wight.
Under the earth ye shall then carefully thus couch,
The roof of your hall your naked nose shall touch ;
Neither great nor small to you will kneel or crouch.
Your goods ye shall forsake if ye be never so loth,
And nothing with you take but such a winding cloth.

[Showing them his own.

Amend thee, man, whilst thou may,
Let never no mirth fordo thy mind ;
Think thou on the dreadful day,
When God shall judge all mankind.
This world is waste, and will away ;
Man, have this in thy mind,
And amend thee whilst thou may.

Amend thee, man, whilst thou art
    here,
Before thou tread another path :
When thou art dead and laid on bier,
Wit thou well thou art too late.
For if all the good that ever thou did,
Were dealt for thee after thy day,
In heaven it would not mend thy state,
So amend thee whilst thou may.
If thou be right royal in rent,
As is the steed standing in stall,
In thy heart know and think
That they are God's goods all.

One of the younger
Disciples.

He might have made thee poor and small
As he that begs from day to day ;
Wit thou well, account give thou shall,
Therefore amend thee whilst thou may.
And if I might with you dwell,
To tell you all my time ;
Full much could I tell
That I have heard and seen,
Of many a great marvel
Such as ye would not ween,

In the pains of hell
There as I have been.
Been have I in woe,
Therefore keep you therefro,
Whilst ye live do so
    If ye will dwell with him
That can to you thus go
    And heal you life and limb.
He is a lord of grace ;
Bethink you in this case,
    And pray him, full of might,
He keep you in this place
    And have you in his sight.   Amen.

[*Here endeth the Lazarus.*]

CHAPTER XVI.—THE PASSION AND THE RESURRECTION

FOR the narrative of the events of the Trial, Crucifixion, and Resurrection of our Lord, we have not
followed one cycle of plays, as that would have
meant the undue prominence of one town, but have
drawn from the gild plays of Chester and from the
Play of Coventry. The first play, *Christ Betrayed*,
is from Chester. Whilst this story is very little
altered, the author has taken the opportunity of
making Malchus seem like the blustering steward of
some lord, of the type which the audience so well
knew. In the second play, *The Trial*, from Coventry,
we meet for the first time Caiaphas and Annas, who
here, as always in the miracle plays, are portrayed in
the mitres and copes of mediæval bishops ; the only
sort of priests of whom the audience was likely to
have knowledge. The next play, like this one, is from
Coventry, and depicts the Crucifixion itself. Although
to us this would seem rather crude and gruesome,

we can imagine it having a great effect on the minds of the audience of those times. The Crucifixion itself is represented in a very simple way, at the expense of losing the Roman soldiers who figure so largely in the original story; but then we must remember that the possibilities of the stage were then rather limited, and the author was chiefly concerned with giving the speeches of Christ and the lament of his mother. The story is continued with the Harrowing of Hell and the Resurrection, both from Chester. The Conquest of Hell, and the release of the souls of the good men of the Old Testament by the descent of Christ into Hell after his death, was a very popular story in mediæval times. It is therefore very interesting to read this elaborate play on a theme which, for various reasons, has quite lost its popularity in the modern world.

The way in which the characters in these plays are modernized is in itself rather interesting. In the days of a public which could not read, there seems little doubt that by presenting Pilate as the governor of a mediæval city, and the priests Caiaphas and Annas as bishops, the players could more easily make their audience realize what manner of men these were. If they had wished to reproduce the costume of the early times, they would have been very hard put to it in those days to find any one competent to tell them how to do so. What they were chiefly out to do was to tell their story as realistically as possible within the limits of the stage; and it is interesting to note by way of comparison that quite recently, when a modern producer acted on this principle in staging *Hamlet* in modern dress, most of the critics who saw the play said that the modern dress made the characters seem much more real and living persons.

The care to preserve the more sacred parts of the play intact from the humorous additions can be compared with Shakespeare's method of writing historical plays. Here the author keeps his real historical characters, like Henry V. or Richard III., fairly close to what people of his time imagined them to be. He gets his fun and his comic relief from characters of his own creation, like Pistol, Nym, Bardolph, and Fluellen; just as his predecessors had got their fun out of less important people like Malchus, or Herod, or Noah's wife.

Mathew 26
John 18: 1-27   I. Christ Betrayed
Luke 22   (The Bakers' Play of Chester.)
Mark 14   SCENE I.   *Outside Jerusalem.*

Jesus. Brethren all, to me right dear,
Come hither to me and you shall hear :
The feast of Easter you know draweth near
And now it is at hand ;
That feast needs keep must we
With very great solemnity,
The paschal lamb eat must we,
As the law doth command ;
Therefore, Peter, look that thou go,
And John with thee shall be also,
Prepare all things that belong thereto,
According to the law.

Peter. Lord, thy bidding do will we,
But tell us first where it shall be,
And we shall do it speedily
And thither will we draw.

Jesus. Go into the city which you do see,
And there a man meet shall ye,
With a waterpot that beareth he,
For so you may him know.
Into what house that he shall go,
Into the same house enter ye also,
And say the master sent ye too
His message for to show ;

Say, " The master to thee us sent,
To have a place convenient,
The paschal lamb there to eat is my intent,
With my disciples all ; "
A fair parlour he will you show,
There prepare all things due,
Where I with my retinue
Fulfil the law we shall.

SCENE II. *A street in Jerusalem.*

*Peter and John shall go and speak with a man bearing
a waterpot, and he shall show them the house of his
master.*

   Peter. All hail, good fellow, heartily !
To thy master's house I pray thee hie,
And we must keep thee company,
Our message for to say.
   The Man. Come on your way and follow me,
My master's house soon shall you see,
Lo, here it is verily,
Say now what you will.
                           [*Then they shall go into the house.*

SCENE III. *Inside the house.*

   Peter. Sir, the master saluteth thee,
And as messengers sent we be,
Therefore we pray thee heartily
Take heed us unto ;
The master hath sent us to thee,
A place prepare for him must we,
The paschal lamb there eat will he,
With his disciples all.
   The Master of the House. Lo, here a parlour all ready
        dight,
With paved floors and windows bright,
Make all things ready as you think right,

And this have you shall.

John. Now, brother Peter, let us hie
The paschal lamb to make ready,
Then to our master will you and I
As fast as we may.

> [*Then they make ready the table.*

Jesus enters.

Peter. Thy commandment, Lord, done have we,
The paschal lamb is made ready.

Jesus. Now, brethren, go to your seat,
The paschal lamb now let us eat,
And then we shall of other things entreat
That be of great effect.
For now you know the time is come
That signs and shadows be all done,
Therefore make haste that we may soon
All figures clean reject.
For now a new law I will begin,
To help mankind out of his sin,
So that he may heaven win,
The which for sin he lost.
And here in presence of you all,
Another sacrifice begin I shall,
To bring mankind out of his thrall,
To help him need I must.

> [*Then Jesus sits down, and John reclineth on his bosom.*

Brethren, I tell you by and by,
With great desire desired have I
This Passover to eat with you truly,
Before my passion ;
For I say to you surely,
My father's will almighty
I must fulfil meekly,
And ever to it be bound.

> [*Then Jesus takes bread, breaks it, and gives it to his disciples, saying :*

This bread I give here my blessing,

Take, eat, brethren, at my bidding,
Believe you will without lesing,
This is my body,
That shall die for all mankind,
In remission of their sin
Hereafter evermore.

[*Then he takes a cup in his hands,
    and raising up his eyes says :*

Brethren, take this with heart free,
For this is my blood,
That shall be shed on the tree,
For more together drink not we,
In heavenly bliss till that we be
To taste that ghostly food.

[*Then he eats and drinks with his
    disciples ; and Judas Iscariot
    shall have his hand in the dish,
    when Jesus says :*

Brethren, forsooth I you say,
One of you shall me betray,
That eateth here with me to-day
In this company.

   Peter. Alas, alas, and welaway !
Who may that be know I nor may,
For I it is not, in good fay,
That shall do such a thing.

[*Then Judas puts his hand in the
    dish.*

   Jesus. Through his deceit I am
    but dead,
That in my cup wets his bread,
Much woe for his wicked rede,
This wretch must suffer, i-wis ;
Well were him had he been unborn,
For body and soul is both forlorn,
That falsely so hath done before,

A Disciple.

Lesing, Lying.

And yet in will is he.

Judas. Lief master, is it I,
That shall do this villainy ?

Jesus. Thou hast rede, Judas, verily,
For surely thou art he ;
That thou shalt do, do hastily.

Judas. Farewell, all this company,
For on an errand I must hie,
Undone it may not be.   [*He goes out.*

Jesus. Brethren, take up this meat anon,
To another work we must be gone,
Your feet shall washen be, each one,
To show all charity ;
And first my feet I will begin,
And wash you all that be herein,
On this deed that you may mind,
And meeker for to be.

              [*Then Jesus girds his body with a linen cloth.*

Peter. Ah, Lord, shalt thou wash my feet ?

Jesus. That do I, Peter, I thee behight ;
The while more thou shalt not wit,
But thou shalt do afterward.

Peter. Nay, Lord, forsooth in no manner
My feet thou may wash here.

Jesus. But I wash thee, withouten doubt
Of joy getst thou no part.

Peter. Nay, Lord, my feet may well be lead ;
But wash my hands and my head.

Jesus. All clean therefore, I do rede,
Thy feet shall washen be.

[*Then he shall wash the feet of each of them in turn, and
        shall wipe them with a cloth.*

Jesus. My little children and my brethren free,
A little while I may with you be,
But thither shall you not go with me,
As I am now in way ;
But this soothly is my bidding,
You love together in all things,

As I before without flinching
Have loved you truly ay ;
So all men may know and see
My disciples that you be,
Falsehood if you always flee,
And love still together.

    Peter. Lord, whither art thou in way ?

    Jesus. Peter, thither as I go to-day,
Come nigh surely thou ne may
This time in no manner a way ;
But thou shalt thither go.

    Peter. Why shall it not be so ?
My life I will put in woe,
And for thy sake be slain.

    Jesus. Peter, I say thee verily,
Before the cock hath crowen three,
Thou shalt forsake my company,
And take thy word again.
Brethren, let not your hearts be sore,
Believe in God evermore,
And in me as you have before,
And care not for this case.
For in my father's house there is
Many dwellings of great bliss,
And thither I will go now, i-wis,
To purvey you a place.
And though I go from you away,
To purvey a place for your pay,
I come again another day,
To take you all with me.
Rise up, and go we hither anon ;
To my prayer I must go
But sit you still every one,
My father while I call.
Wake and have my benison,

Purvey, Provide. The stewards of the king in these days had the
    right to requisition food and fuel for his use in places which
    he visited. This right was called *purveyance*.

For falling into temptation :
The spirit ay to bale is borne,
And the flesh ever ready to fall.

SCENE IV. *The Garden.*

[*Jesus shall go to pray, and the disciples shall sleep.*
 Jesus. Father of heaven in majesty,
Glorify, if thy will be,
Thy son that he may glorify thee,
Now ere hence I wend ;
In earth thou hast given me power,
And I have done with heart free
The work that thou chargëd me,
And brought it to an end.
Thy name have I made men to know,
And spared not thy will to show
To my disciples in a row,
That thou hast given me ;
And now they know verily,
That from the father sent am I,
Therefore I pray thee specially
Save them through thy mercy.
[*Then he shall come to his disciples and find them
    asleep.*
What, sleep you, brethren, all here ?
Rise up, and make your prayer,
Lest temptation have power
To make you for to fall ;
The flesh is, as I said before,
Inclining to sin sore,
And ghost occupied evermore,
Therefore now wake all.
[*Then he shall return to his prayer and, raising his voice,
    he shall say :*
My heart is in great misliking,
For death that is to me coming ;
Father, if I dare ask this thing

Put this away from me;
All thing to thee possible is,
Nevertheless yet in this
At thy will I am, i-wis;
As thou wilt, let it be.

> *[Then he returns to his disciples again.*

You sleep, brethren, yet I see:
Sleep on now all ye;
My time is come taken to be,
From you I must away;
He that hath betrayed me,
This night from him will I not flee,
In sorry time born was he,
And so he may well say.

> *[Then Judas comes thither, with a body of soldiers, with
> lanterns, torches, and arms.*

Jesus. You men, I ask, whom seek ye?
Malchus. Jesus of Nazareth, him seek we.
Jesus. Here, all ready, I am he;
What have you for to say?
Judas. Ah, sweet master, kiss thou me,
For it is long time since I thee see,
And together we will flee,
And steal from them away.
Jesus. Whom seek you, men, with such a breath?
First Jew. We seek Jesus of Nazareth.
Jesus. I said yore, and yet I say,
I am he, in good fay;
Suffer these men to go their way,
And I am at your will.
Malchus. False thief, thou shalt go
To Bishop Caiaphas, and that anon,
Or I shall break thee body and bone,
And thou be too late.
Peter. Thief, and thou be so bold,
My master so for to hold,
Thou shalt be quit an hundredfold,
And onward take thou this!

(2,753)

10

Be thou so bold, as thrive I,
To hold my master here in hye,
Full dear thou shalt it buy !
Be thou the heathen called,
Thy ear shall off, by God's grace
Ere thou pass from this place.
[*Then he shall draw his sword, and shall cut off Mal-
    chus's ear.*
Go now to Caiaphas,
And bid him do thee right.
    Malchus. Out ! alas, alas, alas !
By Coke's bones ! mine ear he has !
Me is betide a hard case,
That ever I came here !
    Jesus. Peter, put up thy sword in hye !
Whosoever with the sword smiteth gladly,
With sword shall perish hastily,
I tell thee, without doubt.
[*Then Jesus shall touch Malchus's ear, and shall cure it.*
    Malchus. Ah ! well is me ! well is me !
My ear is healed well, I see !
So merciful a man as he,
Knew I never none.
    First Jew. Yea, though he have healed thee,
Free of us he shall not be,
But to Sir Caiaphas, as mot I thee,
With us shall he be gone.
    Jesus. As to a thief you come here,
With staves and swords and armour,
To take me in foul manner,
And end your wicked will.
In temple I was with you ay,
No hand on me would you lay ;
But now is come time and day
Your talent to fulfil.
    First Jew. Come on, catiff, to Sir Caiaphas,
Or thou shalt have a hard grace.
Trot upon a prouder space

Thou vile hypocrite !
Thou Beelzebub and Sathanas
Come to help thee in this case,
Both thy hands that thou has
Shall be bound hard.

> [*They go out, taking Jesus with them.*

II. The Trial of Christ   *John 18 : 27-40*

(From the *Play of Coventry.*)

[*Here shall a messenger come into the place, running and crying, " Tidings, tidings ! " and so round about the place : " Jesus of Nazareth is taken ! Jesus of Nazareth is taken ! " and forthwith hailing Annas and Caiaphas, says :*

Messenger. All hail, my lords, princes of priests !
Sir Caiaphas and Sir Annas, lords of the law !
Tidings I bring you, receive them in your breasts ;
Jesus of Nazareth is taken, thereof ye may be glad !
He shall be brought hither to you anon ;
I tell you truly with a great rout,—
When he was taken I was them among,
And there was I near to catch a clout.
Malchus bore a lantern and put him in press,
Anon he had a touch and off went his ear !
Jesus bade his disciple put up his sword and cease,
And set Malchus' ear again as whole as it was ere !
So may I thee, methought it was a strange sight !
When we came first to him, he came to us again,
And asked whom we sought that time of night ?
We said Jesus of Nazareth, we would have him fain.
And he said, " It is I that am here in your sight ; "
With that word were overthrown backwards every one,
And some on their backs lying upright,
But standing upon foot manly there was not one.
Christ stood on his feet as meek as a lamb,

And we lay still like dead men till he bade us rise ;
When we were up, fast hands we laid him upon.

    [*Here bring they Jesus before Annas and Caiaphas.*

The Pageant.

(Showing a performance of the trial before Pilate, as played at Coventry.)

    First Jew. Lo, lo !   Lords, here is the man
That ye sent us for.
    Annas. Therefore we can thee thank then,
And reward ye shall have the more.

Jesus, thou art welcome hither to our presence ;
We paid to thy disciple for thee thirty pence,
And as an ox or an horse we truly thee bought.
Therefore now art ours as thou standest us before ;
Say why thou hast troubled us and subverted our law ?
Thou hast oft concluded us, and so thou hast done more,
Wherefore it were full needful to bring thee a dawe.

> *Caiaphas.* What are thy disciples that followeth
>> thee about ?

And what is thy doctrine that thou dost preach ?
Tell me now somewhat, and bring us out of doubt,
That we may to other men thy preaching forth teach.

> *Jesus.* All times that I have preached, open it was
>> done

In the synagogue or in the temple, where that all
> Jews come :
Ask them what I have said, and also what I have done;
They can tell thee my words, ask them every one.

> *First Doctor.* Sir, this I heard him with his own
>> mouth say,—

" Break down this temple without delay,
And I shall set it up again,
As whole as it was, by the third day."

> *Second Doctor.* Yea, sir, I heard him say also

That he was the Son of God ;
And yet many a fool weeneth so,
I durst lay thereon my head.
Yea, yea ! and I heard him preach many things
And against our law every one ;
Of which it were long to make reckoning,
To tell all at this seel.

> *Caiaphas.* What sayst now, Jesus ? why answerest
>> not ?

Hearest thou not what is said against thee ?
Speak, man, speak !   Speak, thou fop !
Hast thou scorn to speak to me ?

Concluded us, Overcome us in argument.
Bring thee a dawe, Slay thee.   *Seel*, Judgment seat.

Hearest thou not in how many things they thee accuse?
Now I charge thee and conjure, by the sun and the moon,
That thou tell us if thou be God's son!

Jesus. God's son I am, I say not nay to thee!
And that ye shall all see at Doomesday,
When the Son shall come in great power and majesty,
And judge the quick and the dead, as I thee say.

Caiaphas. Ah, out, out! alas! what is this?
Hear ye not how he blasphemeth God?
What needeth us to have more witness?
Here ye have heard all his own word!
Think ye not he is worthy to die?

[*And they shall all shout: " Yes! yes! yes! All we
say he is worthy to die. Yea! yea! yea!"*

Annas. Take him to you and beat him somewhat
For his blaspheming at this seel.

[*Here they shall beat Jesus about the head and the body,
and spit in his face, and pull him down, and set him
on a stool, and cast a cloth over his face.*

First Jew. Ah, fellows! beware what ye do to this
man,
For he prophesy well can.

Second Jew. That shall be assayed by this blow.
What thou, Jesus? who gave thee that?

[*And he shall hit him on the head.*
[*Here shall a serving-maid come to Peter.*

First Maid. What, sirs, how take ye on with this
man?
See ye not one of his disciples how he beholdeth you
then.

[*Here shall the other serving-maid say to Peter:*
Second Maid. Ah! good man meseemeth by thee,
That thou one of his disciples should be.

Peter. Ah! woman, I saw never ere this man,
Since that this wert first begun.

[*And the cock shall crow.*

First Maid. What? thou mayst not say nay, thou
art one of his men,

By thy face well we may thee ken.

Peter. Woman, thou sayest amiss of me ;
I know him not ; so mote I thee.

First Jew. Ah, fellow mine, well met !
For my cousin's ear thou off smote ;
When we thy master in the yard took,
Then all thy fellows him forsook ;

Peter and the Serving-maid.

And now thou mayst not him forsake,
For thou art of Galilee, I undertake.

Peter. Sir, I know him not, by him that made me !
And ye will me believe for an oath,
I take record of all this company,
That I say to you is sooth.

[*And the cock shall crow. And then Jesus shall look
on Peter, and Peter shall weep, and then he shall go
out, saying :*

Peter. Ah! welaway! welaway! false heart, why
        wilt thou not break,
Since thy master so cowardly thou dost forsake?
Alas! where shall I now on earth rest,
Till he of his mercy to grace will me take?
I have forsaken my master and my lord Jesu.
Three times, as he told me that I should do the same;
Wherefore I may not have sorrow enow,
I sinful creature have so much to blame.
When I heard the cock crowing, he cast on me a look,
As who saith, "Bethink thee what I said before."
Alas, the time that I ever him forsook!

Caiaphas. Messenger, messenger!
Messenger. Here, lord, here!
Caiaphas. Messenger, to Pilate in haste thou shalt go,
And say him we commend us in word and in deed;
And pray him that he be at the moot-hall anon,
For we have great matter that he must needs speed.
In haste now go thy way,
And look thou tarry nought.
Messenger. It shall be done, lord, by this day,
I am as quick as thought.

Scene II.

*Here Pilate sitteth on his seat, and the Messenger
kneeleth to him.*

Messenger. All hail! Sir Pilate, that seemly is to
        see!
Prince of all this Jewry, and keeper of the law!
My lord bishop Caiaphas commendeth him to thee,
And prayeth thee to be at the moot-hall by the day's
        dawn.
Pilate. Go thy way, pretty messenger, and com-
        mend me also;
I shall be there in haste, and so thou mayst say:
By the hour of prime I shall come thereto,
I tarry no longer, nor make no delay.

SCENE III.

Here the Messenger cometh again and bringeth his answer.

Messenger. All hail! my lords, and bishops, and princes of the law!
Sir Pilate commendeth him to you, and bade me to you say,
He will be at the moot-hall in haste soon after the day's dawn,
He would ye should be there by prime without longer delay.

Caiaphas. Now well mayst thou fare, my good page;
Take this for thy message.   [*Giving him money.*

Here entereth Judas unto the Jews.

Judas. I, Judas, have sinned and treason have done,
For I have betrayed this rightful blood;
Here is your money again, all and some,
For sorrow and thought I am waxed mad.

Annas. What is that to us? arise thee now,
Thou didst with us a covenant make;
Thou soldest him to us as horse or cow,
Therefore thine own deeds thou must take!

[*Then Judas casteth down the money, and goes and hangs himself.*

Caiaphas. Now, sirs, the night is passed, the day is come;
It were time this man had his judgment;
And Pilate abideth in the moot-hall alone
Till we should this man present;
And therefore go we now forth with him in haste.

First Jew. It shall be done, and that in short space.

Second Jew. Yea, but look if he be bound right well and fast.

Third Jew. He is safe now! go we right a good pace!

SCENE IV.

Here they come to the moot-hall.

Caiaphas. Sir Pilate, take heed to this thing !
Jesus we have before thee brought,
Which our law doth down bring,
And mickle shame he hath us wrought.

    Annas. From this city into the land of Galilee
He hath brought our laws near into confusion,
With his crafts wrought by necromancy,
Shown to the people by false simulation.

    First Doctor. Yea ! yet, sir, another and worst of
        all !
Against Cæsar, our emperor that is so free,
King of Jews he doth him call,
So our emperor's power nought should be !

    Second Doctor. Sir Pilate, we cannot tell half the
        blame
That Jesus in our country hath wrought ;
Therefore we charge thee in the emperor's name,
That he to the death in haste be brought !

    Pilate. What sayst thou to these complaints, Jesus?
These people have thee sore accused,
Because thou bringest up laws new,
That in our days were not used.

    Jesus. Of their accusing me, reck nought,
So that they hurt their souls and no mo.
I have nought yet found that I have sooth,
For my father's will forth I must go.

    Pilate. Jesus, by this, then, I trow thou art a king,
And the son of God thou art also,—
Lord of earth and of all things,—
Tell me the truth, if it be so !

    Jesus. In heaven is known my father's intent,
And in this world I was born ;
By my father I was hither sent,
For to seek that was forlorn.

All that me hear and me believe,
And keep here faith steadfastly ;
Though they were dead I shall them relieve,
And shall them bring to bliss endlessly.

    Pilate. Lo, sirs ! now ye have heard this man,
        what think ye ?
Think ye not all by your reason ?
But as he saith it well may be,
And that should be this occasion.
I find in him no objection
Of error, nor treason, nor no manner guilt.

    First Doctor. Sir Pilate, the law resteth in thee,
And we know verily his great trespass ;
To the emperor this matter told shall be,
If thou let Jesus thus from thee pass !

    Pilate. Take him then after your saw,
And deem him after your law.

    Caiaphas. It is not lawful to us, ye say,
No manner of man to slay ;
The cause why we bring him to thee,
That he should not our king be.
Well thou knowest king we have none,
But our emperor alone.

    Pilate. Sirs, avise you as ye can,
I can find no default in this man.

    Annas. Sir, here is a great record, take heed thereto,
And knowing great mischief in this man ;
And not only in one day or two,
It is many years since he began.
We can tell thee the time where and when,
That many a thousand turned hath he,
And all this people record well can,
From hence into the land of Galilee.

            [*And they shout, " Yea, yea, yea!"*

    Pilate. Sirs, of one thing then give me relation,
If Jesus were born in the land of Galilee,
For we have no power, nor no jurisdiction,
Of no man in that country.

Caiaphas. In Galilee I know that he was born,
I can tell in what place and where.
Against this no man may answer,
For he was born in Bethlehem, Judye.

Pilate. Well, sirs, since I know that it is so,
Lead him to Herod anon present ;
And say I commend me, with word and deed,
And Jesu to him that I have sent.

[*Here they take Jesu and lead him in great haste to Herod.*

SCENE V.

*Herod's palace shall be disclosed, showing Herod in
    state, and all the Jews kneeling, except Annas and
    Caiaphas ; they shall stand.*

First Doctor. Hail, Herod, most excellent king !
We are commended to this presence,—
Pilate sendeth thee by us greeting,
And chargeth us, by our obedience,

Second Doctor. That we should do our diligence
To bring Jesus of Nazareth unto thee,
And chargeth us to make no resistance,
Because he was born in this country.

Annas. We know he hath wrought great folly
Against the law showed present ;
Therefore Pilate sent him unto thee,
That thou shouldst give him judgment.

Herod the King. Now, by Mahound my God of
                          grace !
Of Pilate this is a deed full kind ;
I forgive him now his great trespass,
And shall be his friend withouten end,
Jesus to me that he would send ;
I desired full sore him for to see.
Great ease in this Pilate shall find,
And, Jesus, thou art welcome to me !

First Jew. My sovereign lord, this is the case,
The great falseness of Jesu is openly known :

There was never man did so great trespass,
For he hath almost destroyed our law.

Second Jew. Yea, by false craft of sorcery,
Wrought openly to the people all,
And by subtle points of necromancy,
Many thousands from our law be fall.

Caiaphas. Most excellent king, ye must take heed,
He would destroy all this country, both old and young;
If he ten months more proceed,
By his miracles and false preaching,
He bringeth the people in great folly,
And saith daily among them all,
That he is lord, and of the Jews king,
And the Son of God he doth him call.

Herod. Sirs, all these matters I have heard said,
And much more than ye me tell ;
Altogether they shall be laid,
And I will take thereon counsel.
Jesus, thou art welcome to me ;
I can give Pilate great thanks for his sending ;
I have desired full long thee to see,
And of thy miracles to have knowing.
It is told me thou dost many a wonder thing,
Crooked to go, and blind men to see,
And they that be dead givest them living,
And makest lepers fair and whole to be.
These are wondrous works wrought of thee,
By what way I would know the true sentence.
Now Jesu, I pray thee, let me see
A miracle wrought in my presence.
In haste now do thy diligence,
And peradventure I will show favour to thee ;
For now thou art in my presence,
Thy life and death here lieth in me.

> [*Here Jesus shall speak no word to Herod.*

Jesus, why speakest thou not to thy king ?
What is the cause thou standest so still ?
Thou knowest I may deem all thing,—

Thine life and death lieth at my will !
What ?   Speak, Jesus, and tell me why
This people do thee so here accuse ?
Spare not, but tell me now on high
How thou canst thyself excuse.

   Caiaphas. Lo, sirs ! this is of him a false subtlety,
He will not speak but when he list ;
Thus he deceiveth the people in each degree ;
He is full false, ye verily trust.

The Scourging.

Herod. What, thou unhanged rascal, why wilt thou not speak ?
Hast thou scorn to speak unto thy king ?
Sirs, beat his body with scourges bare,
And assay to make him for to speak !

   First Jew. It shall be done without tarrying.—

[*Here they pull off Jesus' clothes, and beat him with whips.*

   Second Jew. Sirs, take these whips in your hand,
And spare not while they last ;
And beat this traitor that here doth stand,
I trow that he will speak in haste.

[*And when they have beaten him, then Herod saith :*
   Herod. Cease, sirs, I command you by name of the devil of hell !

Jesus, thinkest this good game ?
Thou art strong, to suffer shame ;
Thou hadst rather be beaten lame
Than thy defaults for to tell.
But I will not thy body all spill,
Nor put it here into more pain ;
Sirs, take Jesus at your will,
And lead him to Pilate home again.
Greet him well, and tell him certain,
All my good friendship shall he have ;
I give him power of Jesus, thus ye him say,
Whether he will him damn or save.

First Doctor. Sir, at your request it shall be done,
We shall lead Jesus at your demand ;
And deliver him Pilate unto,
And tell him all as ye command.

[*Here they shall don on Jesus' clothes and over all a
white cloth, and lead him to Pilate.*

Mark 15
Luke 23

John 19
Mathew 27

III. The Condemnation and Crucifixion

Here the Jews bring Jesus again to Pilate.

First Doctor. Sir Pilate, good tidings thou hearest
of me,—
Of Herod the king thou hast good will ;
And Jesus he sendeth again to thee,
He biddeth thee choose, him to save or spill !

Second Doctor. Yea, sir ! all the power lieth now in
thee,
And thou knowest our faith he hath near shent :
Thou knowest what mischief thereof may be,
We charge thee to give him judgment.

Pilate. Sirs, truly ye be to blame,
Jesus thus to beat, despoil, or bind ;
And put him to so great shame ;
For no default in him I find.

Shent, Destroyed.

Nor Herod neither, to whom I sent you,
Default in him could find right none ;
But sent him again to me by you,
As ye know well every one.
Therefore understand what I shall say,
Ye know the custom is in this land,
Of your Easter day that is near at hand,
What thief or traitor be in band,
For worship of that day shall go free away
Without any price.
Now then, one thinketh it were right
To let Jesus now go quite,
And do to him no more despite,—
I would know what ye say.
Sirs, this is mine advice.

         [*Here they all shall cry, " Nay, nay, nay!"*

    First Doctor. Deliver us the thief Barabbas,
That for manslaughter imprisoned was.
     Pilate. What shall I then with Jesus do ?
Whether shall he abide or go ?
     Second Doctor. Jesus shall on the cross be done,
Crucifigatur ! we cry each one.
     Pilate. Sirs, what hath Jesus done amiss ?
     The people cry : Crucifigatur ! we say at once.
     Pilate. Sirs, since at all costs ye will so,
Put Jesus to woe and pain ;
Jesus awhile with me shall go,
I will him examine betwixt us twain.
[*Here Pilate taketh Jesu, and leadeth him aside into the
     council-house.*
     Pilate. Jesus, what sayst now ? let see,
This matter now thou understand ;
In peace thou might be for me,
But for thy people of thy land.
Bishops and priests of the law,
They love thee not, as thou mayst see ;

     Crucifigatur, " Let him be crucified."

And the common people against thee draw.
In peace thou might have been for me,—
This I tell thee plain !
What sayst, Jesus ? why speakest thou not me to ?
Knowest not I have power on the cross thee to do,
And also I have power to let thee forth go !
What hast thou here to sayn ?

   Jesus. On me power thou hast right none,
But that my father hath granted before ;
I came my father's will to fulfil,
That mankind should not spill.
He that hath betrayed me at this time,
His trespass is more than thine.

   First Doctor. Ye princes and masters, take heed and
        see
How Pilate in this matter is favourable ;
And thus our laws destroyed might be,
And to us all unsecurable !

[Here Pilate leaveth Jesus alone, and goeth to the Jews.
   Pilate. Sirs, what will ye now with Jesus do ?
I can find in him but good !
It is my counsel ye let him go,—
It is ruth to spill his blood !

   Caiaphas. Pilate, methinketh thou dost great
        wrong,
Against our law thus to fortify ;
And the people here is so strong,
Bringing thee lawful testimony.

   Annas. Yea, an thou let Jesus from us go,
We will uphold all ;
Thou shalt answer for his trespass,
And traitor to the emperor we shall thee call.

   Pilate. Now then, since ye will no other way,
But in all wise that Jesus must die,
Ontyse, bring me water, I pray thee,
And what I will do ye shall see.

                  [Here one, Ontyse, bringeth water.
As I wash with water my hands clean,

So guiltless of his death I must be.

   First Doctor. The blood of him must be on us,

And on our children after us !

[*And they shout, " Yea, yea, yea ! "   Then Pilate goeth
     again to Jesu, and bringeth him.*

   Pilate. Lo, sirs, I bring him here to your presence,

That ye may know I find in him no offence.

   Second Doctor. Deliver him ! deliver him ! and let
     us go,

On the cross that he were do !

   Pilate. Sirs, would ye your king on the cross I
     would do ?

   Third Doctor. Sir, we say that we have no king but
     the emperor alone.

   Pilate. Sirs, since at all costs it must be so,

We must sit and our office do ;

Bring forth to the bar that are to be deemed,

And they shall have their judgment.

[*Here they shall bring Barabbas to the bar, and Jesu,
     and two Jews, with Jesus standing at the bar
     between them ; and Annas and Caiaphas shall go
     into the council-house where Pilate sitteth.*

   Pilate. Barabbas, hold up thy hand !

For here at thy delivery dost thou stand.

                 [*And he holds up his hand.*

Sirs, what say ye of Barabbas, thief and traitor bold ?

Shall he go free or shall he be kept in hold ?

   First Doctor. Sir, for the solemnity of our Easter
     day,

By our law he shall go free away.

   Pilate. Barabbas, then I dismiss thee,

And give thee licence to go free.

                     [*And he goeth.*

Dysmas and Jesmas there as ye stand,

The law commands you to hold up your hand ;

Sirs, what say ye of these thieves twain ?

   Second Doctor. Sir, they be both guilty, we sayn.

   Pilate. And what say ye of Jesus of Nazareth ?

First Doctor. Sir, we say he shall be put to death !

Pilate. And can ye put against him no trespass ?

Second Doctor. Sir, we will all that he shall be put
upon the cross.

[*And they shall all cry with a mighty voice, saying:
" Yea ! yea ! yea !"*

[*Here Pilate shall rise and go to his house and the
bishops with him ; and the Jews shall cry for joy
with a great noise and they shall put upon Jesus
a cloth of silk, and set him on a stool, and put a crown
of thorns on his head ; and the Jews kneel to Christ,
giving him a sceptre and mocking him, and then
they shall pull off again the purple cloth, and don
again his own clothes ; and lay the cross on his
neck to bear it, and draw him forth with ropes.*

SCENE II

*Then shall they come to women weeping and wringing
their hands.*

First Woman. Alas ! Jesus, alas ! Jesus, woe is me !
That thou art thus despoiled, alas !
And yet never default was found in thee,
But ever thou hast been full of grace.

Second Woman. Ah ! here is a rueful sight of Jesus
so good,
That he shall thus die against the right ;
Ah ! wicked men, ye be more than mad
That do that good Lord so great despite !

[*Here Jesus turneth to the women.*

Jesus. Daughters of Jerusalem, for me weep not,
But for yourself weep and for your children also ;
For the days shall come that they have after sooth
Their sin and their blindness shall turn them to woe !
Then to the hills and mountains they shall cry and
call,
Open and hide us from the face of him sitting on
throne !

Or else overthrow and on us now come fall,
That we may be hid from our sorrowful moan.

[Here Jesus turneth from the women and goeth forth.

A Countryman.

(This kind of dress would be worn by the common
folk and Jews in this play.)

SCENE III

They meet with Simon, the Jews saying to him:

First Jew. Sir, to thee a word of good ;
A man is here thou mayest see,
Beareth heavy of a rood,
Whereon he shall hanged be.
Therefore we pray all thee,
Thou take the cross of the man ;
Bear it with us to Calvary,
And right great thank thou shalt have.

Simon. Sirs, I may not in no degree,—
I have great errands for to do ;
Therefore I pray you excuse me,
And on my errand let me go.

Second Jew. What, fellow ? hast thou scorn
To bear the tree ? when we thee pay !
Thou shalt bear it, hadst thou sworn,
And it were ten times the way !
    Simon. Sirs, I pray you displease you not,
I will help bear the tree ;
Into the place it shall be brought,
Where ye will command me.
[*Here Simon taketh the cross of Jesus and beareth it
    forth. They meet with Veronica.*
    Veronica. Ah, ye sinful people, why fare thus ?
For sweat and blood he may not see.
Alas, holy prophet, Christ Jesus !
Careful is mine heart for thee !
           [*And she wipeth his face with her kerchief.*
    Jesus. Veronica, thy wiping doth me ease.
My face is clean that was black to see.
I shall them keep from all misease,
That look on thy kerchief and remember me !
               [*They lead Jesus forth.*

SCENE IV

*Then shall they pull Jesus out of his clothes, and lay
    them together ; and then they shall pull him down
    and lay him along the cross, and after that nail him
    thereon.*

    First Jew. Come on now here, we shall assay
If the cross for thee be meet ;
Cast him down here in the devil way,
How long shall he stand upon his feet ?
    Second Jew. Pull him down, evil may he thrive !
And give me his arm in haste ;
And anon we shall see
His good days they shall be past !
    Third Jew. Give his other arm to me,—
Another take heed to his feet ;

And anon we shall see
If the bores be for him meet.

Fourth Jew. That I grant, so must I thee ;
Lo, this nail is driven right well and fast.

First Jew. Fast a rope there to his feet,
And draw him down long anon.

Second Jew. Here is a nail for good and great,
I shall drive it through, I make a vow !

[*Here shall they leave off and dance about the cross for a
short space.*

Third Jew. Sirs, set up the cross on its end
That we may look him in the face.

Fourth Jew. Yea, and we shall kneel unto our king
so kind,
And pay him of his great grace !

[*Here when they have set him up, they shall go before
him, saying after each other :*

First Jew. Hail ! King of the Jews if thou be.

Second Jew. Yea, yea ! sir, as thou hangest there
flesh and bones.

Third Jew. Come down now off that tree !

Fourth Jew. And we will worship thee all at once.

[*Here shall poor common folk stand and look upon the
Jews, and the Jews shall make them hang the
thieves.*

First Jew. Come on, ye knaves, and set up these
two crosses right,
And hang up these two thieves anon !

Second Jew. Yea, and in the worship of this worthy
knight,
On each side of him shall hang one !

[*Here the simple men shall set up these two crosses, and
hang up the thieves by the arms ; meanwhile shall
the Jews cast dice for his clothes, and fight and
strive ; and in the meantime shall our Lady come
with three Maries with her, and Saint John with
them, sitting down before the cross ; our Lady
swooning and mourning.*

Mary. Ah, my good lord, my son so sweet !
What hast thou done ?   Why hangest now thus here ?
Is there no other death to thee now meet,
But the most shameful death among these thieves both.
Ah, out on my heart ! why breakest thou not ?
And thou art maiden and mother, and seest thus thy
        child spill !
How mayst thou abide this sorrow and this woeful
        thought ?
Ah, death, death, death ! why wilt thou not me kill ?
                [*Here our Lady shall swoon again.*

Jesus. O father almighty ! maker of men !
Forgive these Jews that do me woe !
Forgive them, father, forgive them then !
For they know not what they do !

First Jew. Yea, what, what ! now here is he
That bade us destroy our temple on a day,
And within days three
He would raise it again in good array.

Second Jew. Now and thou can do such a deed,
Help now thyself, if that thou can ;
And we shall believe on thee without dread,
And say thou art a mighty man !

Third Jew. Yea ! if thou be God's son, as thou
        didst teach,
From the cross come now down !
Then of mercy we shall thee beseech,
And say thou art a Lord of great renown !

Jesmas. If thou be God's son, as thou didst say,
Help now here both thee and us !
But I find it not all in my fay
That thou shouldst be Christ, God's son Jesus.

Dysmas. Go way, fool ! why sayst thou so ?
He is the son of God.   I believe it well !
And sin did he never, lo !
That he should be put this death to.
But we full much wrong have wrought,—
He did never thing amiss !

Now mercy, good Lord ! mercy ! and forget me not
When thou comest to thy kingdom and to thy bliss.

    Jesus. Amen ! amen ! thou art full wise !
That thou hast asked I grant thee.
This same day in paradise
With me thy God thou shalt there be.

    Mary. O, my son, my son ! my darling dear !
What have I offended thee ?
Thou hast spoken to all them that be here,
But not one word thou speakest to me.
To the Jews thou art full kind,
Thou hast forgiven all their misdeed ;
And the thief thou hast in mind,
For once asking mercy, heaven is his meed.
Ah, my sovereign Lord, why wilt thou not speak
To me that am thy mother in pain for thy wrong ?
Ah, heart, heart ! why wilt thou not break ?
That I were out of this sorrow so strong !

    Jesus. Ah, woman, woman, behold thy son !
And thou, John, take her for thy mother !
And, woman, thou knowest that my father of heaven
    me sent
To take this manhood of thee, Adam's ransom to pay ;
For this is the will and to my father's intent,
That I shall thus die to deliver man from the devil's
    prey !
Now since it is the will of my father it should thus be,
Why should it displease thee, mother, now my death
    so sore ?
And for to suffer all this for man I was born of thee,
To the bliss that man had lost, man again to restore.

    [*Here our Lady shall rise and run and embrace the cross.*
    Mary Magdalene. Ah, good lady, why do ye thus ?
Your doleful cheer now profits us sore.
And for the pain of my sweet Lord Jesus,
That he seeth in you, it paineth him more.

    Mary. I pray you all let me be here,
And hang me up here on this tree,

By my friend and son that to me is so dear ;
For where he is, there would I be.

John. Gentle lady, now leave your mourning,
And go with us, now we you pray !
And comfort our lord at his departing,
For he is almost ready to go his way.

[*Here they shall take our Lady from the cross ; and here
shall Pilate come with Caiaphas and Annas and all
their train ; and they shall come and look on Christ,
and Annas and Caiaphas shall scornfully say :*

Caiaphas. Lo, sirs, lo ! behold and see,
Here hangeth he that helped many a man ;
And now if he God's son be,
Help now himself if that he can.

Annas. Yea, and if thou king of Israel be,
Come down off the cross among us all !
And let thy God now deliver thee,
And then our king we will thee call !

[*Here shall Pilate ask for pen and ink and a tablet.
And he shall write :* HIC EST JESUS NAZARENUS
REX JUDÆORUM. *Then he shall go up a ladder,
and set the tablet above Christ's head.*

Caiaphas. Sir Pilate, we marvel at this,
That you write him the king of the Jews.
Therefore we would that ye should write thus,
That he named himself king of Jews.

Pilate. That I have written, written it is,
And it shall be for me, i-wis.

[*And they shall all go forth again, and Jesus shall say :*
Jesus. Heloy ! Heloy ! Lama zabathany !
My father in heaven on high,
    Why dost thou me forsake ?
The frailty of my mankind,
With strong pain beginneth to pain,
Ha, dear father, have me in mind,
    And let death my sorrow slake !

Hic est, etc., " This is Jesus of Nazareth, king of the Jews."
Heloy ! etc., Cf. Matt. xxvii. 46, and Mark xv. 34.

Second Jew. Methinketh he thus doth call Eli;
Let us go near and espy,
And look if he come privily,
    From cross him down to bring.

Jesus. So great a thirst did never man take
As I have, Man, now for thy sake;
For thirst asunder my lips do crack,——
    For dryness they do cleave.

Third Jew. Your thirst, Sir Hoberd, for to slake,
Aysel and gall here I thee take,
What, methinketh a face ye make,——
    Is not this good drink?
To cry for drink ye had great haste,
And now it seemeth it is but waste,——
Is not this drink of good taste?
    Now tell me how ye think!

Fourth Jew. Aloft, Sir Hoberd, now ye be set,
We will no longer with you let,
We greet you well in the new gett
    And make at you a face.

First Jew. We greet you well with a scorn,
And pray you, both even and morn,
Take good eye to our corn,
    And scare away the crow.

Jesus. *In manus tuas, Domine!*
Holy father in heavenly see,
I commend my spirit to thee,
    For here now endeth my fest!
I will go slay the fiend, that freak,
For now mine heart beginneth to break,
Words more shall I none speak.
    Nunc consummatum est!

Mary. Alas, alas, I live too long,
To see my sweet son in pains so strong,

Hoberd, Perhaps a clown.	*Aysel*, Vinegar.
Face, Grimace.	*Gett*, Fashion.
In manus, etc., Into thy hands, O Lord!	
Nunc, etc., Now it is finished.	

As a thief on cross doth hang,
    And never yet did he sin !
Alas, my dear child to death is dressed,
Now is my care well more increased.
Ah, mine heart with pain is pressed !
    For sorrow mine heart doth cleave.

John. Now, dear lady, therefore I you pray,
From this doleful dolour wend we our way,
For when this sight ye see not may,
    Your care may wax more light.

Mary. Now since I must part him fro,
Yet let me kiss ere that I go,
His blessed feet that suffer woe,
    Nailed on this tree.
So cruelly with great despite,
Thus shameful was never man dight,
Therefore in pain my heart is pight.
    All joy departed from me.
        [*Here she falls to the ground as if half-dead.*

John. Now, blessed maid, come forth with me !
No longer this sight that ye see,
I shall you guide in this country,
    Where that it pleaseth you best.

Mary. Now, gentle John, my son's darling !
To God's temple thou me bring,
That I may pray God with sore weeping
    And mourning what is past !

IV. The Harrowing of Hell

(The Cooks and Innkeepers' *Play of Chester.*)

*First of all there shall be in hell a great light, produced
by some subtle means ; and then Adam shall speak.*

Adam. O Lord and sovereign Saviour,
Our comfort and our counsellor,
Of this light thou art author,
I see well in sight ;

This is a sign thou wilt succour
Thy folks that lie in great languor,
And of the devil be conqueror,
As thou hast ever behight.
Me thou madest, Lord, of clay,
And gave me Paradise in to play,
But through my sin, the truth to say,
Deprived I was therefro ;
And from that weal put away,
And here hath longed, the truth to say,
In thirstiness both night and day,
And all my kind also.
Now by this light that I now see,
Joy is coming, Lord, through thee,
And of thy people thou hast pity,
To put them out of pain ;
Surely it may none other be,
But now thou hast mercy on me,
And my kind, through thy power,
Thou wilt restore again.

    Isaiah. Yea, surely, this same light
Comes from God's son almight,
For so I prophesied aright
When that I was living :
Then I to all men behight,
As I ghostly saw in sight,
These words that I shall to my might
Rehearse without tarrying.
The people, I said that time express,
That went about in the darkness,
See now a full great lightness,
As you do now each one ;
Now is fulfilled my prophecy,
That I, the prophet, Ysaie,
Wrote in my book that will not lie,
Whoso will look thereon.

    Simeon. And I, Simeon, truth to say,
For when Christ child was, in good fay,

In temple I him took,
And as the Holy Ghost that day
Taught me ere I went away,
These words I said to God's pleasure
That men may find in book,
Nunc dimittis servum tuum, Domine, secundum, verbum
tuum in pace.
There I prayed, without falsehood,
That God will let me be in peace,
For he is Christ that comen was,
I have both felt and seen,
That he had ordained for man's heal,
Joy to the people of Israel,
Now is it won, that very weal,
To us without a doubt.

    John the Baptist. Yea, Lord, I am that prophet
        John
That baptized thee in flood Jordan,
And preached to every nation,
To warn of thy coming ;
To bring the people to salvation
By merit of thy bitter passion,
Through faith and penance to have remission,
And with thee to have dwelling.
And with my finger I show express
Mercy concluded righteousness,
Therefore these words I do rehearse,
With honour unto thee.

    Seth. And I, Seth, Adam's son, am here,
That living went, withouten doubt,
To ask at Paradise a prayer
Of God, as I shall say ;
That he would grant an angel on high
To give me oil of his mercy,
To anoint my father in his annoy,
In sickness when he lay.

Nunc dimittis, etc., "Lord, now lettest thou thy servant depart
    in peace, according to thy word."

To me appeared Michael,
And bade me sorrow never a deal,
And sad weeping nor prayers fell
That grant me not to seek ;
Nor of that oil might I have none,
Made I never so much moan,
Till five thousand years were gone
And five hundred eke.

   David. Ah, high God, and king of bliss,
Worshipped be thy name, i-wis ;
I hope that time now comen is,
Delivered to be of languor,
And take out thy folk every each one,
For the years all be come and gone,
Since mankind came first here.

[*Then Satan, sitting on his throne, shall speak to the
    demons :*

   Satan. Hell-hounds all, that be here,
Make your bow with boast and noise,
For to this fellowship in fear
There hies a fearsome freke.
Jesus, that is God's son,
Comes he hither with us to dwell,
On him now ye you wreak.
A man he is fully in fay,
For greatly death he dread to-day,
And these words I heard him say,
" My soul is thirst to death."
Such as I made halt and blind,
He has healed them to their kind,
Therefore this boaster look that you bind
In bale of hell breath.

   Second Demon. Sir Sathanas, what man is he,
That should deprive thee of thy power ?
How dare he do against thee,
And dread his death to-day ?

Freke, Man, warrior.

Greater than thou he seems to be,
For degraded of thy degree
Thou must be soon, well I see,
And deprivëd of thy prey.

Third Demon. Who is he so stiff and strong
That so masterly comes us among,
Our fellowship as he would take ?
But thereof he shall fail.
Wete he us with any wrong,
He shall sing a sorry song,
But on thee, Satan, that it belongs,
And his will ought avail.

Satan. Against this shrew that sits here
I tempted the folk in foul manner,
Aysel and gall for his dinner
I made them for to dight ;
And since to hang him on rood tree,
Now he is dead right so through me,
And to hell, as you shall see,
He comes anon in height.

Second Demon. Sir Sathanas, is not this that seer,
That raised Lazarus out of the fire ?

Satan. Yea, this is he that would conspire
Anon to reave us all.

Third Demon. Out, out ! Alas, alas !
Here I conjure thee, Sathanas,
Thou suffer him not come in this place,
For aught that may befall.

Second Demon. Yea, verily, and he come here,
Passed is clean our power,
For all this fellowship in fear,
Have when away he would ;
For at his commandment,
Lazarus, that with us was lent,
Despite our teeth he went,
And him might we not hold.

Aysel, Vinegar.

*Then Jesus shall come, and there shall be a mighty
noise ; and Jesus shall say without :*

 Jesus. Open up hell gates anon,
You princes of pain every one,
That God's son in may go,
And the king of bliss.

 Second Demon. Go hence, hypocrite, out from this
   place,
Or thou shalt have a sorry grace,
For all thy boast and thy menace
These men thou shalt miss.

 Satan. Out, alas ! what is this ?
Saw I never so much bliss,
Towards hell come, i-wis,
Since I was warden here.
My masterdom fares amiss,
For yonder a stubborn fellow is,
Right as wholly hell were his,
To rob me of my power.

 Third Demon. Yea, Sathanas, thy sovereignty
Fails clean, therefore thou flee,
For no longer in this see
Here shalt thou not sit :
Go forth, fight for thy degree,
Or else our prince thou shalt not be,
For now passes thy power,
And hence thou must flit.

    [*Then Satan rises from his seat.*

 Satan. Out, alas ! I am undone,
My might fails verament,
This prince that is now present
Will take from me my prey.
Adam, by my enticement,
And all his blood, through me were spoiled ;
Now hence they shall be all called,
And I in hell for ay.

 David the King. I, King David, now well may say

My prophecy fulfilled is in fay,
And now shows in sight verily,
And soothly here is seen ;
I taught men this here in my life day
To worship God by all way,
That hell gates he shall affray,
And won that his hath been.

Jesus. Open up, hell gates, yet I say,
You princes of pain that be present,
And let the king of bliss this way,
That he may fulfil his intent.

[*Here the gates of hell burst asunder, and Jesus
    cometh in.*

Satan. Stay, what is he that king of bliss ?

David the King. The Lord, the which almighty is,
In war no power like to his,
Of all bliss is greatest king,
And to him is none like, i-wis,
As is soothly seen by this,
For men that sometime did amiss,
To his bliss he will us bring.

[*Here Jesus doth take out Adam.*

Jesus. Peace to thee, Adam, my darling,
And eke to all thy offspring,
That righteous were in earth living,
From me you shall not sever ;
To bliss now I will you bring,
There you shall be without ending,
Michael, lead these men singing
To bliss that lasteth ever.

Michael. Lord, your will shall be done ;
Come forth, Adam, come with me :
My Lord upon the rood tree
Your sins hath all forbought ;
Now shall you have liking and lee,
And be restored to your degree,

Lee, Salvation.

That Satan with his subtlety
From bliss to bale had brought.

[*Then Michael shall lead forth Adam and the saints
to paradise, and there shall meet them Enoch and
Elijah and the saved Thief.*

  Satan. Out, alas ! now goes away
All my prisoners and my prey,
And I myself may not start away,
I am so straitly tied !
Now comes Christ, sorrow I may,
For me and my maynee alway,
Never since God made the first day,
Were we so sore afraid.

        [*Here must Adam speak to Enoch and Elijah.*

  Adam. Sirs, what manner of men be ye,
That bodily meet us as I see,
That dead came not to hell as we,
Seeing all men damned were ?
When I trespassed, God bade me
That this place closed should be
From earthly men to have entry,
And yet I find you here.

  Enoch. Sir, I am Enoch the sooth to say,
Put in this place to God's pay,
And here have lived ever since ay
At liking all my fill ;
And my fellow here, in good fay,
Is Elijah the prophet, see you may,
That taken was in this array,
As it was God's, will.

  Elijah the Prophet. Yea, bodily death, believe thou me,
Yet never suffered we,
But here ordained we are to be,
Till Antichrist come ;
To fight against us shall he,
And slay us in this holy city,
But surely in days three
And an half we shall rise.

Adam. And who is this that comes here,
With cross on shoulder in such manner ?
Thief. I am that thief, my father dear,
That hung on rood tree.
For I believed without a doubt
That Christ might save us both at once :
To him I made my prayer,
The which was granted me,
When I see signs verily
That he was God's son, sooth to say,
To him devoutly did I pray,
In his region when I came,
That he would think on me alway ;
And he answered and said, This day
In Paradise thou shalt with me play
Hitherward anon.
Then he betaught me this tokening,
This cross upon my back hanging,
To Michael angel for to bring,
That I might have entry.
Adam. Now go we to bliss both old and young,
To worship God all-willing ;
And thitherward I rede we sing
With great solemnity.
[*Then they all go forth, singing, " Te Deum laudamus,
te Dominum confitemur."*

V. The Resurrection

Mathew 28
Mark 16
Luke 24
John 20

(The Skinners' *Play of Chester.*)

SCENE I. *Pilate's Hall.*

Pilate. You lords and ladies, so lovely and fair,
You ken, you know knights of kind,
Hearken all hitherward my hestes to hear,
For I am most fairest and freshest to find,

Te Deum, " We praise thee, O God, we acknowledge thee to be
the Lord."

And most mighty I am of estate.
For I am prince peerless,
Most royal man of riches,
I may deal and I may dress,
My name is Sir Pilate.
For Cæsar, prince most of power,
Honoured my estate and my degree,
When that he sent Jesus to me,
To deliver him to the dead ;
They cried on me all with one voice,
The Jews on me made great noise ;
I gave them all leave to hang him on cross,
This was through Jews' rede.
I dread ye lest he will us grieve,
For that I saw I may well believe ;
I saw the stones begin to cleave,
And dead men up can rise.
In this city all about
Was none so stern nor so stout,
That up looked for great doubt,
They were so sore aghast.
And therefore, Sir Caiaphas, yet I dread
Lest there be peril in that deed ;
I saw him hang on rood and bleed
Till all his blood was shed ;
And when he should his death take,
The weather waxed wondrous black ;
Light, thunder, and earth began to quake,
Thereof I am adread.
 Caiaphas. And this was yesterday about noon.
 Pilate. Yea, sir bishop, this is one,
To speak therefore we have to done,
For I let bury him full soon,
In tomb of stone ;
And therefore, sirs, among us three,
Let us ordain and oversee
If there any peril be,
Ere we hence go.

Annas. I saw him and his company
Raise men with sorcery,
That long before were dead ;
For and there be any more such left,
Which can of such witchcraft,
If that body be from us reft,
Advise you well, I rede.

Caiaphas. Yea, Sir Pilate, I tell you right,
Let us ordain many a hard knight,
Well armed to stand and fight,
With power and with force ;
That no shame to us befall.
Let us ordain here among us all,
And true men to us call,
To keep well the corpse.

Pilate. Now, by Jesus that died on rood,
Methink your counsel is wondrous good,
The best man of kin and blood,
Anon, look ye not cease.
And my knights, stiff and stern of heart,
You be bold men and smart ;
I warn you now with wordës short,
For with you I have to do.

First Knight. Sir, we be here, all and some,
As bold men, ready bound
To drive your enemies all down ;
While that we may stand,
We be your knights every one ;
Faintness in us there shall be none,
We will wreak us upon thy foes,
Wherever he may be found,
And for no dread that we tarry.

Pilate. That I am well to understand,
You be men doughty of hand,
I love you without lack ;
But that prophet that was done and drawn,
Through the recounting of your law,
But yet something we stand in awe,

Of words that he spake.
Forsooth this heard I him say,
That he would rise the third day ;
Now surely and he so may,
He hath a wondrous sign.

    Second Knight. Yea, let him rise if that he dare !
For and I of him may be aware,
He bode never a worse chance
Ere that he went away.
I helped to slay him ere while,
When is he to do us more guile ?
Nay, it is no peril ;
My head there dare I lay.

    Third Knight. Yet let him quicken hardly,
While my fellows here and I
May awake and stand him by,
He 'scapeth not uncaught ;
For and he once heave up his head,
But that he be soon dead,
Shall I never eat more bread,
Nor nevermore be sought.

    First Knight. Have good day, sir, we will be gone :
Give us our charge each one.

    Pilate. Now farewell, the best of blood and bone,
And take good heed unto my saw.
For as I am a true Jew,
If that you any treason show,
There is none of you shall esue,
But he shall be to drown.

    Scene II.   *The Sepulchre.*

    Second Knight. Now, fellows, we be charged hie,
Our prince hath sworn that we shall die
Without any prophecy,
Or any other in charge ;

    Esue, Escape.

But if we do as the wise,
I rede we right well advise,
Though he be bold he shall not rise,
But one of us beware.
 Third Knight. Sir, the most wit lieth in thee,
To ordain and to oversee ;
You be the eldest of us three,
And man of most renown ;
The tomb is here at our hand,
Set us there as we shall stand,
If that he rise we shall find
To beat him adown.
 First Knight. And I shall now first set us so,
If that he rise and would go,
One of us or else two,
Shall see of his uprise ;
Stand thou here, and thou
  here,
And I myself in middle
  mere :
I trow our heart will not
  fear,
But it were stoutly wist.
[*Then two Angels shall come
  and shall sing : " Christ
  is risen from the dead,"
  and then Christ shall
  rise, and after their song
  is finished shall speak.*
 Christ. Earthly man that
  I have wrought,
Awake out of thy sleep ;
Earthly man that I have bought,
Of me thou have no keep.
From heaven man's soul I sought,
Into a dungeon deep.

The Resurrection.

Mere, Boundary.

I am very prince of peace,
And king of free mercy;
Who will of sins have release,
On me they call and cry.
And if they will of their sins cease,
I grant them peace truly,
And thereto a full rich mass—
In bread my own body.
I am very bread of life,
From heaven I light and am sent,
Who eateth that bread, man or wife,
Shall live with me withouten end.
And that bread that I you give,
Your wicked life for to amend,
Becomes my flesh through your belief,
And doth release your sinful band.
And whosoever eateth that bread
In sin or wicked life,
He receives his own death,
I warn both man and wife.

[*Then the two Angels, after Christ has risen, shall sit in the tomb, one at the head, and one at the feet.*

First Knight. Out, alas! where am I?
So bright about is here by,
That my heart wholly
Out of my breast is shaken;
So foul feared with fantasy
Was I never in such annoy,
For I wot not truly
Whether I were asleep or waking.

[*Then he rouses one of his companions.*

Second Knight. Where art thou, Sir Bachelor?
About me is wondrous clear,
Wit me wants withouten doubt,
For fearder I never was.
To remove far or near,
Me fails might and power,

My heart in my body here
Is hoven out of my breast.

                 [Then they waken the Third Knight.

   First Knight. Yea, we are cursed verily,
For Jesus is risen, well wot I,
Out of the sepulchre mightily,
And thereof I have in mind ;
And as dead here can I lie,
Speak might I not, nor spy
Which way he took truly,
My eyes they were so blind.

   Third Knight. Alas ! what is this great light
Shining here in my sight ?
Marred am I, main and might,
To move I have no main.
These two beasts that are so bright,
Power have I none to rise aright,
Me fails with them for to fight,
Would I never so fain.

   Second Knight. Yea, I will creep forth on my knee,
Till I this peril passëd be,
For my way I may not see,
Neither earth nor stone.
Yea, in wicked time we
Nailed him on the rood tree,
For, as he said, in days three
Risen he is and gone.

   Third Knight. Hie we fast we were away,
For this is God's son verray ;
Strive with him may we nay,
That master is and more.
I will to Caiaphas by and by,
The sooth openly for to say :
Farewell, sirs, and have good day,
For I will go before.

   First Knight. To linger here were no boot,
For needs to Sir Pilate we must,
And tell him crop and root

So soothly as we wist ;
For and the Jews knew as well as we,
That he was risen through his power,
Then should the last errand be
Worse than the first.

[*Then they go unto Pilate.*]

Scene III. *Pilate's Hall.*

Second Knight. Hearken, Sir Pilate, the sooth to
        say,
Jesu that was on Friday slain,
Through his might is risen again,
This is the third day.
There came no power to him fetch,
But such a sleep he on me set,
That none of us might him let
To rise and go his way.
    Pilate. Now, by the oath I have to Cæsar sworn,
If that you have privily
Sold him to his company,
Then are you worthy for to die
Right in your own wrong.
    Third Knight. Now, by the order I bear of knight,
He rose up in the morning light,
By virtue of his own might :
I know it very well.
He rose up, as I say now,
And left us lying I wot ne'er how,
All bemazed in a swoon,
As we had been stuck swine.
    Pilate. Fie, thief ! fie, traitor !
Fie on thee ! thy trust is full bare !
Fie, fiend ! fie, feature !
Hie hence fast !   I rede thou fare.
    First Knight. That time that he his way took,
Durst I neither speak nor look,
But for fear I lay and quoke,

And lay in sound dream :
He set his foot upon my back,
That every limb began to crack ;
I would not abide such another shake,
For all Jerusalem.

    Pilate. Fie, villain ! fie, hound !
Fie on thee, thou tainted dog !
What ! lay thou still in that place,
And let that flatterer go on, the rogue ?
Sir Caiaphas and Sir Annas,
What say you to this trespass ?
I pray you, sirs, in this case,
Advise me of some rede.

    Caiaphas. Now, good sir, I you pray,
Hearken to me what I you say,
For much avail us it may,
And do after my spell.
Pray them now, sir, pardye,
As they love well thee,
Here as they stand all three,
To keep well our counsel.

    Annas. Sir Bishop, I say to you verament,
Unto your counsel I fully assent ;
This foolish prophet, that we all so rent,
Through his witchcraft is stolen away ;
Therefore let us call our council together,
And let us conclude to the whole matter,
Or else our laws are done for ever hereafter.

    Pilate. Now in good faith, full woe is me,
And so I trow be all ye,
That he is risen thus privily
And is from us escaped ;
Now I pray you, sirs, as you love me,
Keep this counsel and privity
Unto our council, and till we
Have heard how he escaped.

          [*Then he gives them money and they go away.*

SCENE IV. *The Sepulchre.*

There shall come women weeping and seeking Jesus.

Mary. Alas, now lorn is my liking ;
For woe I wander, and hands wring ;
My heart in sorrow and in sickness
Is sadly set and sore.
That I most loved of all things,
Alas, is now full low lying ;
Why am I, Lord, so long living,
To lose thy pleasant sight ?

Mary, mother of James. Alas ! well away ; is went
My help, my heal from me is rent ;
My Christ, my comfort, that me hent,
Is faded now in clay.
Mighty God omnipotent,
Thou give them hard judgment,
That my sovereign so have shent,
For so I may well say.

Mary Magdalene. Sister, which of us every one
Shall remove this great stone
That lieth my sweet Lord upon,
For move it I ne may.

Mary, mother of James. Sister, miracle is it none :
It seems to me as he were gone,
For on the sepulchre sitteth one,
And the stone away.

Mary Salome. Two children here I see sitting,
All of white is their clothing,
And the stone besides lying :
Go we near and see.

[*Then they go and look into the sepulchre.*

First Angel. What seek you, women, here
With weeping and unliking cheer ?
Jesus, that to you was dear,
Is risen, believe you me.

Second Angel. Be not afraid of us in fear.

For he is gone, withouten doubt,
As he before can you lere,
Forth into Galilee.

 First Angel. This is the place, so be appeased,
That Jesus our Lord was in laid,
But he is risen, as he said,
And hence went away.

 Second Angel. Hie you for ought that may befall,
And tell his disciples all,
And Peter also say you shall,
There find him that you may.

 Mary Magdalene. Ah ! hie we fast for anything,
And tell Peter this tiding,
A blissful word we may him bring,
Sooth if that it were.

 Mary, mother of James. Yea, walk thou, sister, by
     one way,
And we another shall assay
Till we have met with him to-day,
My worthy lord so dear.

 [*Then they go away and walk about the garden a little.*

Scene v. *The Garden.*

The women meet the disciples, Peter and John.

 Mary Magdalene. Ah ! Peter and John, alas ! alas !
There is befallen a wondrous case ;
Some man my Lord stolen has,
And put him I wot not where.

 Peter. What, is he removed out of the place
In the which he buried was ?

 Mary Magdalene. Yea, surely, all my solace
Is gone and is not there.

 John. Peter, go we thither anon,
Running as fast as we can,
To look who hath removed the stone,
And whether he be away.

Peter. Abide, brother, sweet John,
Lest we meet with any one ;
But now I see no other one,
To run I will assay.

> [*Then they run together.*

SCENE VI. *The Sepulchre.*

John runs before Peter, but they enter not the sepulchre.

John. Ah, Peter, brother in good fay,
My Lord Jesu is away !
But his sudary, sooth to say,
Lying here I find.
By itself, as thou see may,
Far from all other clothes it lay ;
Now Mary's words are sooth very,
As we may have in mind.
Peter. Yea, but, as God keep me from woe,
Into the sepulchre I will go,
To look if it be very so,
As Mary to us can say.

> [*Then they shall go into the sepulchre.*

Ah ! Lord blessed be thou ever and ay,
For as thou told me and others mo,
I find thou hast overcome our foe,
And risen out, in good fay.

> [*Then Peter speaks in lamentation.*

Ah, Lord, how shall I do for shame,
That hath deserved so much blame,
To forsake thy holy name,
To meet with thee by any way.
I that in penance and great annoy
My sweet Lord forsook thrice,
Save endless hope of his mercy,
Thereto trust I may,
For were it not his great grace,

Sudary, A linen cloth, kerchief.

And sorrow of heart that in me was,
Worse I were than Judas was,
My Lord so to forsake.
   John. Peter, comfort thee in this case,
For surely my Lord Jesu accepted has
Great repentance for thy trespass,
My Lord in heart will take.
Go we seek Jesu anon in hie,
One way thou, another way I.
   Peter. Yea, well I hope through his might
My penance shall him please.

[They go forth.

Mathew 25:31-4[6]
Revelation 6-21

CHAPTER XVII.—DOOMESDAY

In the Middle Ages people were much attracted by the
idea of the Last Judgment. We often find it painted
in frescoes on the walls of their churches. At Lutter-
worth in Leicestershire, at Salisbury, at St. Albans,
and at many other places, we find this subject prominent in the inside of parish churches. As a play it
does not seem to modern eyes a very promising subject, but it was made the closing scene of the mystery
cycle. It offered scenic possibilities, which were eagerly
developed.

We have already read of the earthquake produced
for this scene at Coventry. It was the custom also
for the saved souls to be clad in white and the
damned souls in black, so that the audience could
more easily distinguish. It is interesting to find this
practice referred to by Shakespeare, who seems to have
known his mysteries pretty well. In *Henry V.* the
Boy asks: "Do you not remember, a' saw a flea stick
upon Bardolph's nose, and a' said it was a black soul
burning in hell fire?" For the present purpose we
have taken a short version of the story, from the *Play
of Coventry*, as this is quite enough to give a good idea

of the scene. Unfortunately, it has lost the closing
speech, after the devils have carried off the damned
souls. Other more complicated versions, such as the
one at Chester, contain righteous Popes, condemned
Popes, just kings, condemned merchants, and so on.

Doomesday

*Here begins the Day of Judgment. Jesus descends with
Michael and Gabriel, the archangels ; and Michael
says :*

Surgite ! all men arise !
Venite ad judicium !
For now is set the high justice,
And hath assigned the day of doom.
Come now quickly to this great assize,
Both great and small, all and few,
And of your answer now take heed
What ye shall say when that ye come,
Your answer for to tell.
For when God shall examine you,
There is no help of any excuse,
The truth full truly he will hear
And send you to heaven or hell.
   Gabriel. Both pope and prince, and priest with
       crown,
King and Cæsar, and knights so keen,
Quickly come your excuses to make,
For this shall be the day of ire.
Neither poor nor rich of great renown,
Nor all the devils in hell that are
From this day forth shall hide you more,
For all your deeds here shall be seen
Openly in sight.

Venite, etc., " Come ye to the judgment ! "

DOOMESDAY

Whoever is found in deadly guilt,
He were better to be hid;
In endless hell he shall be destroyed,
His deeds his death shall cause.

[*All the Souls shall rise from their graves, whilst the
earth quakes and the world is consumed by fire.
As they rise they cry: "Ah, ah, ah! Ah, ah,
ah!"*]

The Souls. Ah, ah, ah! cleave asunder, ye clods
of clay,
Asunder ye break and let us pass,
Now may our song be, welaway,
That ever we sinned in deadly trespass.

All the Demons cry: Harrow and out! What shall
we say?
Harrow, we cry, out and alas!
Alas, harrow! Is this that day,
To endless pain that us must pass?
Alas! harrow and out, we cry!

All the risen Souls cry: Ah, mercy, Lord, for our
misdeeds,
And let thy mercy spring and spread!
But alas! we bide in dread
It is too late to ask mercy.

God appears on high, and speaks: Venite, benedicti,
My brethren all,
Ye children dear,
Come hither to me to mine hall;
All my suitors and servants to be,
And all the foul worms from you fall.
With my right hand I bless you here.
My blessing burnished you as bright as beryl,
As crystal clear it cleanseth you clean,
All filth from you fade.
Peter, to heaven's gates wend thou and go,
The locks thou loosen and them undo,

Venite, benedicti, "Come, ye blessed ones."

(2,753)

13

My blessed children thou bring me to
Their hearts for to glad.

Peter. The gates of heaven I open this tide :
Now welcome, dear brethren, to heaven i-wis ;
Come on, and sit on God's right side,
Where mirth and melody never may miss.

The saved Souls. On knee we creep, we go, we glide,
To worship our Lord that merciful is ;
For through his wounds that be so wide
He hath brought us to his bliss.
Holy Lord, we worship thee !

God. Welcome ye be in heaven to sit,
Welcome, from me shall ye never flit,
So sure of bliss ye shall be yet,
To mirth and joy welcome ye be !

The damned Souls. Ah, ah ! Mercy we cry and crave,
Ah ! mercy, Lord, for our misdeed !
Ah ! mercy, mercy, we rubbe ! we rave !
Ah ! help us, good Lord, in this need !

God. How would ye, wretches, and mercy have ?
Why ask ye mercy now in this need ?
What have ye wrought your souls to save ?
To whom have ye done any merciful deed,
Mercy for to win ?

First Devil. Mercy? nay, nay, they shall have wreck,
And that on their foreheads witness I take,
For there is written with letters black,
Openly, all their sin.

God. To hungry and thirsty that asked in my name,
Meat and drink would ye give none ;
Of naked men had ye no shame,
Ye would not clothe men in any prison ;
Ye had no pity on sick or lame,
Deeds of mercy would ye never do.
These works do you fordo.
For your love's sake I was rent on the cross,
And for your sake I shed my blood.
When I was so merciful and so good,

Why have ye wrought against my will ?
    Second Devil. I find here written on thy forehead,
Thou wert so stout and set in pride,
Thou wouldst not give a poor man bread,
But from thy door thou wouldst him chide.
    Third Devil. And in thy face I here do read,
That if a thirsty man come any tide,
Drink from him thou wouldst ever hide ;
On covetousness was all thy thought.
    Fourth Devil. The sin of sloth thy soul shall curse,
Mass nor matins wouldst thou none hear,
To bring the dead man thou wouldst not went,
Therefore thou goest to endless fire.
    The damned Souls. Ah, mercy, lord, mighty of power,
We ask thy mercy and not by right.
Now after our deed, so us requite ;
We have sinned, we are to blame.

CHAPTER XVIII.—THE CONVERSION OF SAINT PAUL

WE have now traced out something of the development which took place from the first clumsy plays of
the Cornish type ; and for a fully developed play we
cannot do better than read the *Conversion of Saint
Paul*, a play of which the place of performance is
unfortunately unknown. We feel that here is something more like a play as we know it. It is divided
up into well-defined scenes. Annas and Caiaphas
appear once more as bishops, and bless their champion
Saul as he sets out for Damascus. Our old friend the
raging Devil appears, but there seems reason to believe
that he was an addition to the original play, put in to
please the public which liked its roaring demons and
its fire of hell. Already in these days producers were
offering what the public wanted. The poet himself,

or probably after the earliest performances some one
to represent him, comes in before each scene to recite
a short prologue.

The Conversion of Saul

ACT I

Acts 9: 1-31

Enter the Poet as Prologue.

Poet. Rex, glory, king omnipotent,
Redeemer of the world by the power divine,
And Mary, that pure virgin, queen most excellent,
Which bare the blessed babe Jesu, that for us suffered
      pain,
Unto whose goodness I do incline,
Beseeching that chord of his piteous influence
To preserve and govern this worshipful audience.
Honourable friends, beseeching you of licence,
To procede our process, we may, under your correction,
The conversion of St. Paul, as the Bible gives experi-
      ence,
Who list to read the book *Acta Apostolorum*
There shall he have the very notition ;
But as we can we shall see us redress
Briefly with your favour beginning our process.

                              [Exit Prologue.

SCENE I. *Jerusalem*

*Here enters Saul, goodly beseen, in the best wise like an
adventurous knight.*

Saul. Most feared man I am living upon the earth,
Goodly beseen with many a rich garment ;
My peer alive, I trow, is not found
Through the world from the Orient to the Occident.
My fame is best known under the firmament ;

Acta Apostolorum, The Acts of the Apostles.

I am most dread of people universal,
They dare not displease me most noble.
Saul is my name I will that ye notify,
Who conspireth the disciples with threat and menace ;
Before the prince of priests most high and noble
I bring them to punishment for their trespass.
We will them not suffer to rest in no place,
For they go about to preach and give examples,
To destroy our laws, synagogues, and temples.
By the god Belial, I shall make progress
Unto the princes, both Caiaphas and Annas,
Where I shall ask of them in sureness
To pursue through all Damascus and Lybia ;
And thus we shall soon after then
Bring them, that so do live, into Jerusalem
Both man and child that I find of them.

                        [Here enter Caiaphas and Annas.

Noble prelates and princes of regalty,
Desiring and asking of your benign worthiness
Your letters and epistles of most sovereignty,
To subdue rebellions that will of frowardness
Against our laws rebel or transgress,
Nor will not incline but make objection,
To pursue all such, I will do protection.

  Caiaphas. To your desire we give perfect sentence,
According to your petitions that ye make postulation,
Because we know your true diligence,
To pursue all those that do reprobation
Against our laws by any regardation ;
Wherefore shortly we give in commandment
To put down them that be disobedient.

  Annas. And by these letters that be most reverent,
Take them in hand, fully agree thereto ;
Constrain all rebels with our whole assent,
We give you full power so to do.
Spare not hardly for friend and foe
All those ye find of that life in this realm,
Bound look ye bring them into Jerusalem.

[Here Saul receiveth their letters.

Saul. This precept here I take in hand,
To fulfil after your wit both,
Where I shall spare within this land
Neither man nor woman, to this I make an oath;
But to subdue I will not be loth.
Now follow me, knights and servants true,
Into Damascus as fast as ye can go.

    First Knight. Unto your command-
      ment I do obeisance;
I will not gainsay nor make delation;
But with good mind and hearty pleasance
I shall you succeed and make perambula-
    tion
Throughout Damascus with all delecta-
    tion;
And all that rebel and make resistance
For to oppress I will do my diligence.

    Second Knight. And in me shall be no
      negligence,
But to this precept myself I shall apply,
To do your behest with all convenience
With any frowardness or obstinacy.
None shall appear in me but verily
With all my mind I you assure
To resist those rebels I will do my trust.

A Bishop.
(Caiaphas or
Annas.)

    Saul. Truly to me it is great consolation
To hear this report that ye do advance.
For your sapiential wits I give commendation,
Ever at my need I have found you constant;
But knights and servants that be so pleasant,
I pray you anon my palfrey ye bring
To speed my journey without letting.*

    Servant. Ho, ostler, ho! A peck of oats and a bottle
      of hay
Come here apace, or I will to another inn.

    * For acting purposes it might be advisable to omit the remain-
ing part of this scene.

What, ostler, why cometh not thy way ?
Hie ye faster, I beshrew thy skin.

 Ostler. I am no ostler nor ostler's kin
But a gentleman's servant, I would you know ;
Such crabbish words do ask a blow.

 Servant. I cry you mercy, sir. I wist well somewhat
   ye were
Either a gentleman or a knave, methinketh by your
   physiognomy ;
If one look you in the face that never saw you ere,
He would think ye were at the next door by.
In good faith, I thought you had been an ostler verily.

 Ostler. In faith, thou never sawest me till this day.
I have dwelt with my master this seven year and more.
Full well I have pleased him, he will not say nay,
And much he maketh of me therefore.

 Servant. By my truth, then, be ye changed to a new
   lore ;
A servant ye are, and that a good,
There is no better looketh out of a hood.

 Ostler. Forsooth, a hood I used to wear.
Full well is it lined with silken cloth,
It keepeth me from the cold, that the wind doth me
   not harm,
Neither frost nor snow that I thereby doth set.

   [*Here cometh the First Knight to the stable groom.*
 First Knight. Now, stable groom, shortly bring forth
   away
The best horse, for our lord will ride.

 Ostler. I am full ready, here is a palfrey ;
There can no man a better bestride
He will conduct our lord and guide.
Through the world he is sure and able
To bear a gentleman he is easy and profitable.

   [*Here the Knight cometh to Saul with a horse.*
 First Knight. Behold, Sir Saul, your palfrey is come,
Full goodly horse beseen, as it is your desire
To take your voyage through every region.

Be not in doubt, but well speed your matter,
And we be as your servant with glad cheer ;
To give attendance we will not gainsay,
But follow you where ye go by night and day.

    Saul. Unto Damascus I make progression,
To pursue all rebels, who are froward and obstinate
Against our laws by any transgression,
With all my diligence myself I will prepare.
Concerning my purpose to oppress and separate,
None shall rejoice that doth offend,
But utterly be reproved with mind and intent.

    [*Here Saul rideth forth with his servants out of the place.*

    Caiaphas. Now Saul hath taken his worthy voyage,
To pursue the rebels of what degree they be,
He will not suffer to reign nor have passage
Within all this region we be in, certain
Wherefore I commend his goodly dignity
That he thus alway taketh in hand
By his power to govern thus all this land.

    Annas. We may live in rest by his consolation ;
He defendeth us, wherefore we be bound
To love him entirely with our hearty affection,
And honour him as champion at every time.
There is none such living upon the ground
That may be like him nor be his peer,
From east nor west, far nor near.

ACT II

    The Poet (as prologue). Honourable friends, we be-
        seech you of audience
To hear our intention and also our process ;
Upon our matter be your favourable licence
Another part of the story we will redress.
Here shall be briefly shown, with all our business
At this pageant, St. Paul's conversion.
Take ye good heed and thereto give affection.

SCENE I. *The road to Damascus*

Here cometh Saul riding with his servants.

Saul. My purpose to Damascus fully I intend
To pursue the disciples my life I apply ;
For to break down the churches thus I condescend.
None will I suffer that they shall edify
Perchance our laws, that might thereby ;
And the people also turn and convert,
Which should be great heaviness unto my heart,
Nay, that should not be but laid apart.
The princes have given me full protestation,
All that I find they shall not start,
But bound to Jerusalem with furious violation
Before Cæsar, Caiaphas, and Annas' presentation.
Thus shall be subdued those wretches of that life,
That none shall enjoy, neither man, child, nor wife.

[*Here cometh a whirlwind with great tempest, and Saul
falleth down off his horse. That done, God speaketh
in heaven.*

God. Saul, Saul, why dost thou me pursue,
It is hard to prick against the spur ;
I am thy saviour that is so true,
Which made heaven and earth and each creature :
Offend not my goodness, I will thee now cure.

Saul. O Lord, I am afeard. I tremble for fear.
What wouldst thou I did ? Tell me here.

God. Arise, and go thou with glad cheer
Into the city a little beside,
And I shall thee succour in every dere
That no manner of ill shall betide.
And I will there for thee provide
By my great goodness what thou shalt do.
Hie thee fast thither, as thou mayst go.

Saul. O merciful God, what aileth me ?
I am lame, my leg is taken me fro,
My sight likewise I may not see ;

I cannot tell whither to go,
My men have forsaken me also.
Whither shall I wend, or whither shall I pass,
Lord, I beseech thee, help me of thy grace.

    First Knight. Sir, we be here to help thee in thy
        need,
With all our affiance we will not cease.

    Saul. Then to Damascus I pray you me lead
In God's name according to my promise.

    Second Knight. To put forth your hand look ye
        dress ;
Come on your way we shall you bring
Into that city without tarrying.

                    [*Here the Knights lead forth Saul.*

Scene ii. *Damascus*

Christ appeareth to Ananias.

    God. Ananias, Ananias, where art thou, Ananias ?
    Ananias. Here, Lord, I am here truly.
    God. Go thy way and make thy course
As I shall assign thee by my advice,
Into the street that is called Straight,
And in a certain house of warrantise
There shall ye find Saul in humble wise,
As a meek lamb, that a wolf before was named.
Do my behest, be nothing ashamed.
He lacketh his sight, by my punishment constrained.
Praying unto me, I assure thou shalt him find,
With my stroke of pity sure he is pained
Wanting his sight, for he is truly blind.

    Ananias. Lord, I am afeared, for always in my mind
I hear so much of his furious cruelty,
That for speaking thy name to death he will put me.

    God. Nay, Ananias, nay, I assure you
He will be glad of thy coming.

    Ananias. Ah, Lord, but I know of a certain

That thy saints in Jerusalem to death he doth bring;
Many ills of him I have been kenning,
For he hath the power of the princes all
To save or spill, do which he shall.

    God. Be nothing adread, he is a chosen vessel,
To me assigned by my godly election
He shall bear my name before the king and children
        of Israel ;
By many sharp showers suffering correction,
A great doctor of benign complexion,
The true preacher of the high divinity,
A very pinnacle of the faith I assure thee.

    Ananias. Lord, thy commandment I shall fulfil,
Unto Saul I will take my way.

    God. Be nothing in doubt for good nor ill.
Farewell, Ananias, tell Saul what I do say. [*Exit God.*

    Ananias. Blessed Lord, defend me, as thou best may.
Greatly I fear his cruel tyranny,
But to do thy precept myself I shall apply.

Scene iii. *Another part of Damascus*

    First Knight. I marvel greatly what it doth mean
To see our master in this sad state.
The wondrous great lights that did so shine
Smote him down off his horse to the ground,
And methought that I heard a sound
Of one speaking with voice delectable
Which was wonderful mirable.

    Second Knight. Certainly this light was fearful to
      see,
The sparks of fire were very fervent,
It inflamed so grievously about the country
That, by my truth, I thought we should have been
      burnt.
But now, sirs, let us relent
Again to Caiaphas and Annas to tell this chance
How that befel to us no grievance.

Scene IV.

[Here Saul is in contemplation.

Saul. Lord, of thy comfort much I desire,
Thou mighty king of Israel, prince of pity,
Who me hast punished as thy prisoner,
That neither eat nor drank these days three,
But, gracious Lord, for thy visitation I thank thee ;
Thy servant shall I be as long as I have breath,
Though I therefore should suffer death.

[Here cometh Ananias to Saul.

Ananias. Peace be in this place and goodly mansion,
Who is within speak in Christ's holy name.

Saul. I am here, Saul come on God's benison.
What is your will tell me without blame ?

Ananias. From Almighty God certainly to thee am
  I sent,
And Ananias men call me where as I dwell.

Saul. What would ye have, I pray you me tell ?

Ananias. Give me your hand for your avail,
For as I was commanded by his gracious sentence
And bade thee be steadfast for thou shalt be hale,
For this same cause he sent me to thy presence,
Also he bade thee remember his high excellence
By the same token that he did thee mete,
Toward the city when he did appear in the street ;
There mayst thou know his power celestial,
How he disposeth everything as him list,
Nothing may withstand his might essential
To stand upright or else down to thrust.
That is the message that he doth thee send.

Saul. His mercy to me is right welcome ;
I am right glad that it is thus.

Ananias. Be of good cheer and perfect jubilation.
Put forth thy hand and go with me ;
Again to thy sight here I restore thee.

Saul. Blessed Lord, thanks to you ever be,
The mist is fallen from mine eyes twain.

Where I was blind and could not see,
Lord, thou has sent me my sight again.
From sobbing and weeping I cannot refrain,
My pensive heart full of contrition,
For my offences my body shall have punition,
And where I have used so great persecution
Of thy disciples through all Jerusalem
I will aid and defend their predication
That they did teach in all this realm.
Wherefore, Ananias, at the watery stream
Baptize me, heartily I do thee pray
Among your number that I elect and chosen may be.

    Ananias. Unto this well of much virtue
We will us hie with all our diligence.

    Saul. Go you before, and after I follow,
Lauding and praising our Lord's benevolence.
I shall never offend his high magnificence,
But always observe his precepts and keep,
For my great unkindness my heart doth weep.

    Ananias. Kneel ye down upon this ground,
Receiving this christening with good intent,
Which shall make you whole of your deadly wound
That was infected with venom nocent.
It purgeth sin, and fiend's powers so fraudulent
It putteth aside ; where this doth attain
In every place he may not obtain.
I christen you with mind full perfect,
Receiving you into our religion
Ever to be steadfast and never to flit,
But ever constant without variation.
Now is fulfilled all our observation,
Concluding thou mayst it ken
In nomine patris et filii et spiritus sanctus.   *Amen.*

    Saul. I am right glad as fowl in flight
That I have received this blessed sacrament.

Nocent, Harmful.
In nomine, etc., "In the name of the Father, the Son, and the
    Holy Ghost.   Amen."

I fully assent at your request
To be guided and rule as ye will have me,
Even at your pleasure as ye think best.
Go your way, I will follow
Into what place ye will me lead.

ACT III

Enter the Poet as Prologue.

Poet. The might of the Father, potential deity,
Pursue this honourable and worshipful congregation
That here be present of high and low degree.
We shall proceed with all our delectation
If it will please you to give audience favourable.
Hark wisely thereto, it is good and profitable.

SCENE I. *Jerusalem*

First Knight. Noble prelates, take heed to our sen-
tence,
A wonderful chance fell and did betide
Unto our master Saul when he departed hence,
Into Damascus purposed to ride.
A marvellous light from the element did glide
Which smote down him to ground both horse and man
With the fearfullest weather that ever I in came.
  Second Knight. It ravished him and his spirit did
benumb,
A sweet dulcet voice spake him unto
And asked wherefore he made such persecution
Against his disciples and why he did so.
He bade him into Damascus to Ananias go
And there he should receive baptism truly,
And now clean against our laws he is truly.
  Caiaphas. I am sure this tale is not true.
What ! Saul converted from our law !
He went to Damascus for to pursue

All the disciples that did withdraw
From our faith ; this was his saw.
How say ye, Annas, to this matter ?   This is a marvel-
    lous chance.
I cannot believe that it is of assurance.

    Annas. No, Caiaphas, my mind truly do I tell
That he will not tell in no manner wise ;
But rather to death put and expel
All miscreants and wretches that do arise
Against our laws by any enterprise.
Say the truth without any cause fraudulent,
Or else for your tales ye be like to be shent.

    First Knight. Else our bodies may be put to pain.
All that we declare, I saw it with mine eye,
Nothing offending but truly do justify.

    Caiaphas. By the great God I do marvel greatly ;
If this be true that ye do tell,
He shall repent his rebellious traitory,
That all shall beware of his falseness ;
We will not suffer him to obtain doubts
For many perils that might betide
By his subtle means on every side.

    Annas. The law is committed to our advisement,
Wherefore we will not see it decay
But rather uphold it, help and augment,
Lest any reproof to us fall may
From Cæsar the emperor ; by night and day
We shall to such matters hark and attend,
According to the laws our wits to spend.

Scene ii. *In Hell*

Here enters a Devil with thunder and fire.

    Devil. Ho, ho, behold me, mighty prince of the parts
    infernal.
Next unto Lucifer I am in majesty ;
By name I am called the god Belial.

None of more might nor of more excellence ;
My power is principal and now of most sovereignty,
In the temple and synagogue who denieth me to
    honour
My bishops through my motion they will him soon
    devour.
I have moved my prelates Caiaphas and Annas
To pursue and put down, by power royal
Through the cities of Damascus and Lybia,
All such as to worship the high God supernal
Their death is conspired without any favour at all.
My bishops have chosen one most vigorous
Them to pursue, whose name is Saul.
[*Here shall enter another devil called Mercury, amid fire,
    coming in haste, crying and roaring.*

    Mercury. Ho, out, out ! Alas this sudden chance
Well may we bewail this cursed adventure.
    Belial. Mercury, what aileth thee ? Tell me thy
    grievance.
Is there any that has wrought us displeasure ?
    Mercury. Displeasure enough, thereof ye may be
    sure,
Our law at length it will be clean down laid,
For it is decayed sore, and more will, I am afraid.
    Belial. How can that be ? It is not possible.
Consider, thou fool, the long continuance.
Decay, quotha, it is not creditable
Of false tiding thou makest here utterance.
Behold how the people have no pleasaunce
But in sin, and to follow our desire.
What is the tidings ? Tell out ; let us see
Why art thou amazed so, declare before us
What fury is fallen that troubleth thee thus.
    Mercury. Ho, out, out ! He that I most trusted to,
And he that I thought would have been to us most
    special,
Is now of late turned, and our cruel foe.
Our special friend, our chosen Saul,

Is become servant to the high God eternal.

Belial. Ho, out, out ! What, have we lost
Our darling most dear whom we loved most ?
But is it out truth that thou dost here specify ?

Mercury. It is so, undoubted ; why should I feign ?
But let us provide for remedy shortly.
Wherefore let us both by one assent
Go to the bishops and move them privily,
That by some subtle means they may cause him to die ;
Then shall he in our law make no disturbance,
Nor hereafter cause us to have grievance.

Belial. Well said, Mercury, thy counsel is profitable.
Ho, Saul, thou shalt repent thy unstableness.
Thou hadst been better to have been conformable
To our law ; for this death doubtless
It is conspired to reward thy falseness.

[*Here they shall vanish away with a fiery flame and a
    tempest.*

SCENE III. *Damascus*

Here appeareth Saul in a disciple's dress.

Saul. The Lord that is the shaper of the sea and the
        land,
And hath wrought by his word all things at his will,
Save this seemly company that here sitteth or stands,
For his great mercy, that we do not perish.
Grant me, good lord, thy pleasure to fulfil,
And send me such speech as I the truth say,
My intentions profitable to move if I may.
Well-beloved friends, there be seven mortal sins
Which be proved principal and chiefest of poisons.
Pride that of bitterness all bale begins,
Withholding all faith it feedeth and foisons,
As Holy Scripture beareth plain witness.
Of all vices and folly pride is the root ;
Humility may not reign, nor yet endure ;
Pity, alack, that is flower and boot,

Is expelled where pride hath succour.
Good lord, give us grace to understand and persevere
Thy word as thou biddest to fulfil ever.
This is my counsel, bear thee not too high,
But dread alway sin and folly,
Wrath, envy, covetousness, and sloth,
Vanity and vain glory, and false idleness.
Wherefore I rehearse this with mine own mouth,
Keep clean your body from all taint of sin,
Steady your sight, and look ye not stunt,
For of a certainty I know at a brunt
That the eye is ever the messenger of folly.

    The Priest's Servant. What, is not this Saul that took
        his voyage
Into Jerusalem, the disciples to oppress ?
Bound he would bring them if any did rage
Upon Christ ; this was his process.
To the princes of peace he said, doubtless,
Through all Damascus and also Jerusalem,
Subdue all temples that he found of them.

    Saul. Yes, certainly Saul is my proper name,
That had in power the full dominion.
To hide it from you it were a great shame
And mortal sin, as in my opinion,
Unto Cæsar and priests of the religion,
And temples of the Jews that be very hideous
Against almighty Christ, the king so precious.

    Servant. To Annas and Caiaphas ye must make your
        recourse ;
Come on your way and make no delacion.

    Saul. I will you follow, for better or worse,
To the princes of priests with all delectation.

SCENE IV.   *The Temple in Damascus*

    Servant. Holy priest, of high protestation
Here is Saul, look on him wisely,
He is another man than he was verily.

Saul. I am the servant of Jesus almighty,
Creator and maker of sea and land,
Who is king omnipotent of heaven's glory,
Chief comfort and solace both to free and bound,
Against whose power nothing may stand.
Emperor he is both of heaven and hell,
Whose goodness and grace all things doth excel.

[He is led away.

Caiaphas. Upon my heart, this is great admiration
That Saul is thus marvellously changed ;
I trow he is bewitched by some conjuration,
Or else the devil on him is avenged.
Alas, to my heart it is descended
That he is thus taken from our religion ;
How say ye, Annas, to this conversion ?

Annas. Full marvellously, as in my conception,
This wonderful case how it befel ;
To see this chance so suddenly done
Unto my heart it doth great ill.
But for his falseness we shall him pay,
By mine assent to death we will him bring,
Lest that more mischief of him may spring.

Caiaphas. Ye say very true, we might it all rue ,
But shortly in this we must have advisement,
For that against us he may not continue ;
Peradventure, of Cæsar we may then be shent.

Annas. Nay, I had rather in fire he were burned,
Than of Cæsar we should have displeasure
For such a rebel and subtle false traitor.

Caiaphas. We will command the gates to be kept
about,
And the walls surely on every side
That he may not escape, nowhere, out,
For die he shall, I assure you indeed.

Annas. This traitor rebellious, evil must he suffer
That doth this unhappiness against all.
Now every custodian keep well his wall.

Servant. The gates are shut ; he cannot escape.

Every place is kept well and sure
That in no wise he may, till he be taken,
Get out of the city by any conjecture.
Upon the caitiff and false traitor
Look ye be avenged with death mortal,
And judge him as ye list to what end he shall.

Scene v. *Damascus, in the Prison*

An Angel. Holy Saul, I give you monition
The princes of Jews intend certain
To put you to death ; but by God's provision
He wills ye shall live longer and obtain ;
And after thy death thou shalt reign
Above in heaven, with our Lord's grace.
Convey yourself shortly to another place.

 Saul. The Lord's pleasure ever must be done
Both in heaven and in hell as his will is.
In a bearing basket or a leap anon
I shall me convey with help of the disciples,
But I trust in our Lord that is my succour
To resist their malice and cruel fury.

The Epilogue

 Poet. Thus leave we Saul within the city,
The gates kept by commandment of Caiaphas and
  Annas,
But the disciples in the night over the wall, truly
As the Bible saith *dimiserunt eum in sporta,*
And Saul after that in Jerusalem *vera*
Joined himself and there accompanied
With the disciples where they were unfeigned.
This little pageant thus conclude we
As we can, lacking literal science ;
Beseeching you all of high and low degree

 Dimiserunt, etc., " Let him down in a basket."—Acts ix. 25.

Our simpleness to hold excused, and licence
That of rhetoric have no intelligence,
Committing you all to our Lord Jesu,
To whose laud ye sing—*Exultet celum laudibus*.

CHAPTER XIX.—THE MORALITY OF WISDOM

DURING the fifteenth century it became the custom to introduce into the mysteries characters of a new type —allegorical figures, we should call them—men and women who personate ideas like Justice and Mercy, Bribery and Despair. This idea would seem a little dull to us, but to the mind of the men of that time Gluttony or Faith was not pictured as the *idea* of over-eating and drinking, or as the *idea* of steadfast belief. Gluttony was imagined as a man having a tremendous meal ; and Faith as a man being constant under trials. Consequently these characters made themselves very much at home on the fifteenth-century stage.

In the poetry of the time there is also the same tendency. As early as the days of Edward III. had appeared *Piers Plowman,* a poem by William Langland, which told of the sad condition of England. Here the cause of all evil was bribery, which is represented in the person of Lady Meed, who ingratiates herself with the king. He suggests that she should marry Conscience. Conscience exposes her faults and refuses to wed her. Hereupon the king orders Reason to be sent for. Reason arrives with his supporters Wit and Wisdom. The latter are won over by Wrong, who has Lady Meed's help, but Reason stands firm and urges the king to follow Justice. The king agrees, and begs Reason to live with him ever afterwards.

Exultet, etc., " Let the heaven ring with his praise."

At first these abstract qualities were added to older plays. *Death, Truth, Mercy, Peace,* and other allegorical figures, were introduced into various parts of the *Play of Coventry.* But naturally it was not long before men got the idea of plays in which the action was entirely performed by abstract qualities, and to this kind of play we usually give the name of *morality.* Some of the early moralities are difficult to read, but a good early example is this account of *how Lucifer tempts the Mind, Will, and Understanding of Man to sin.* Lucifer is still here the half-comic devil of the mystery play. The scene of the play is naturally very vague, as it is hard to imagine when such people as the Soul, Understanding, or Wisdom would exist. We have taken the liberty of reducing this play to less than half its original length, as some of these abstract figures, in spite of their shadowy nature, had no fear of making their presence felt by long and tedious speeches.

A Morality of Wisdom

Scene 1

First entereth Wisdom in a rich purple cloth of gold, with a mantle of the same, ermined within, having about his neck a royal hood furred with ermine, having upon his head a wig with bows, and a beard of gold sipres curled. A rich imperial crown thereupon set with rich stones and pearls ; in his hand an orb of gold with a cross thereupon, and in his right hand a royal sceptre.

Wisdom. If ye will know the propriety
And the reason of my name imperial,
I am called by them that on earth be
Everlasting Wisdom, to my splendour equal ;

Sipres, Galingale, a kind of reed.

Which name accordeth best in especial,
And most to me is convenient.

[*Here entereth the Soul as a maiden, in a white cloth of
    gold, greatly purfled with miniver; a mantle of
    black; thereupon a wig like to Wisdom, with a rich
    chaplet laced behind, hanging down with two knots of
    gold and side tassels; she kneels down to Wisdom.*

Soul. From my youth this have I sought
To have my spouse most specially;
For a lover of your shape I am wrought
Above all health and beauty that ever was sought.
I have loved Wisdom as for my light,
For all goodness with him he brought,
In Wisdom I was made all beauty bright;
Of your name the high felicity
No creature knoweth full exposition.
    Wisdom. I am founder's light without comparison
Of stars above all the disposition,
Forsooth of light the very brightness,
Mirror of the divine domination
And the image of his goodness.
Wisdom is better than all earthly preciousness,
And all that may desired be   .
Is not in comparison to my likeness.
The length of the years in my right side be,
And in my left side riches, joy, and prosperity.
Lo, this is the worthiness of my name?
    Soul. Ah, sovereign Wisdom, if your benignity
Would speak of love, that were a game.
    Wisdom. Of my love to speak it is mirable.
Behold now, Soul, with joyful mind,
How lovely I am, how amiable
To be greeted and kissed by mankind;
To all clean Souls I am full gracious,
And ever present where they be.
They that of the heavy burden of sin have cure
My love discharged and purifieth clean;

It strengtheneth the mind, the soul made pure,
And giveth wisdom to them that perfect be.
Who taketh me to spouse may verily ween
If above all things he love me specially,
That rest and tranquillity he shall see
A day in surety of joy perpetual.

    Soul. O worthy spouse and sovereign fair,
O sweetest friend, our joy, our bliss,
To your love who doth repair
All felicity in that creature is.
What may I give to you again for this ?
O creator, lover of your creature ;
Though by our frailty we do amiss,
Your great mercy ever spareth violence.
O sovereign Wisdom ! *sanctus sanctorum !*
What may I give to your most pleasure ?

    Wisdom. I ask nought else of all this substance ;
Thy clean heart, thy meek obedience,
Give me that, I am content.

    Soul. Ah, sovereign joy, my heart's affiance !
The fervour of my love to you I represent ;
That maketh my heart, your love so fervent ;
Teach me the schools of your divinity.

    Wisdom. Desire not to savour of knowledge too
        excellent,
But dread and conform your will to me,
For it is a helpful discipline that in wisdom may be :
The dread of God, this is beginning ;
The weeds of sin it maketh to flee,
And sweet virtuous herbs in the soul spring.

[*Here enter five virgins in white kirtles and mantles, with
    wigs and chaplets, and sing :* "Nigra sum, sed
    formosa filia Ierusalem, sicut tabernacula cedar,
    et sicut pelles Salmonis."

Sanctus sanctorum, "Holy of holies."
Nigra sum, etc., "I am black but comely, O daughter of Jerusalem,
    like the tabernacle of cedar, and like the skin of Solomon"
    (*cf.* Song of Solomon i. 5).

Soul. Ye daughters of Jerusalem me not blame
For this shadow I bear of humanity
That as the tabernacle of cedar without is black
And within, and the skin of Solomon full of beauty.

Wisdom. Thus all the souls that in this life be
Standing in grace be like to this.
Ah, *quinque prudentes!* your five wits!
Keep you clean, and ye shall never deface,
Your God's image never shall destroy,
For the clean soul is God's resting-place.
Three powers every Christian soul has
Which are applied to the trinity.

Mind. All these here, lo, before your face,
Mind,

Will. Will,

Understanding. And Understanding, we three.

Wisdom. Ye three declare then this
Your signification and your propriety.

Mind. I am Mind, that in the soul is
The very figure of the Deity,
When in myself I have mind, and see
The benefits of God and his worthiness.

Will. And I of the soul am the Will
Of the Godhead likeness, and a figure
With goodwill no man may spill,
Nor without good will of bliss be sure.

Understanding. The third part of the soul is Under-
standing ;
For by Understanding I behold what God is,
In himself beginning without beginning,
And end without end that shall never miss.
Incomprehensible in himself he is,
His works in me I cannot comprehend.
Of all creatures he is lovëd sovereign,
For he is God of each creature,
And they be his people, that ever shall reign,

Quinque prudentes, Five wits.

In whom he dwelleth as in his temple sure.

Wisdom. Lo, these powers in one soul be,
Mind, Will, and Understanding ;
By Mind of God the father knowledge have ye ;
By Understanding of God the Son, ye have knowledge ;
By Will which turned into love burning,
God the Holy Ghost that called is love,
Not three Gods but one God in being :
Thus each clean soul is similitude of God above.
By Mind faith in the father have we,
Hope in our Lord Jesu by Understanding,
And by Will in the Holy Ghost charity.

Soul. Sovereign Lord, I am bound to thee.
When I was nought, thou made me thus glorious ;
When I perished through sin, thou savedst me ;
When I was in great peril, thou kept me, Christ ;
When I erred, thou restored me, Jesus ;
When I was ignorant, thou taughtst me truth ;
When I sinned, thou corrected me thus ;
When I was heavy, thou comfortedst me by pity ;
When I stand in grace, thou holdest me that time ;
When I fall, thou raisest me mightily ;
When I go well, thou art my guide ;
When I come, thou receivest me lovingly ;
Thou hast anointed me with the oil of mercy ;
Thy benefits, Lord, be innumerable ;
Wherefore praise endless to thee I cry,
Recommending me to thy endless power durable.

[*Here they go out ; the five wits going before and singing,
the Soul next, and her followed Wisdom, and after
him Mind, Will, and Understanding.*

SCENE II

*Lucifer entereth in a devil's array without, and within
(i.e. underneath) as a proud gallant.*

Lucifer. Out, harrow, I roar !
For envy I am lost,

My place to restore.
God hath made men,
I shall tempt them so sore.
For I am he that sin began ;
Lucifer am called.
Presuming in God's sight,
Wherefore I am lowest in hell ;
In reforming of my place, is dight
Man, whom I have in most despite
Ever casting me with them for to fight
In that heavenly place that he should not dwell.
I am wily now as then
The knowledge that I had, yet I ken.
I know all complexions of men
Whereto he is most disposed,
And therein I tempt him ay when
I mar his minds till they wan ;
Then woe is him, God him began ;
Many an holy man by me is mazed.
Of God man is the figure,
His similitude, his picture
Most glorious of any creature
That ever was wrought
Which I will disfigure
By my false conjecture ;
If he list to my report
I shall tempt him to nought.
In the soul three parts, i-wis,
Mind, Will, Understanding of bliss,
Figure of the Godhead, I know well this ;
And the flesh of man that is so changeable
That will I tempt, as I guess.
Though that I pervert, sin none is
But if the soul consent to miss.
For in the will of the soul be the deeds damnable.
To the mind of the soul I shall make suggestion
And bring his Understanding to delectation
So that his Will make confirmation.

That I am sure and know,
The deed shall follow, of damnation ;
Then of the soul the Devil hath domination.
I will go make this examination,
To all the devils of hell I make a vow.
But for to tempt man in my likeness
I would bring him to great fearfulness ;
I will change me into brightness
And so him to beguile.
Sin I shall show as perfectness ;
And virtue, prove it wickedness :
Thus under colours all things perverse
I shall never rest till the soul I defile.

[*Here Lucifer disappeareth, and cometh in again as a
      goodly gallant.*

Scene III

Enter also Mind, Will, and Understanding.

Mind. My mind is ever on Jesu
That endued us with virtue ;
His doctrine to follow
Ever I purpose.
    Understanding. Mine Understanding is, in truth,
That with faith he did us renew ;
His laws to pursue
Is sweeter to me than the savour of the rose.
    Will. And my will is his will verily,
That made us his creatures so specially ;
Yielding unto him laud and glory
For his goodness.
    Lucifer. Ye fond fathers, founders of folly,
Ye will perish, or ye it aspy
The Devil hath accombred you express.
Mind, mind, sirs, have mind of this !
    Mind. He is not idle that with God is.
    Lucifer. No, sir, I prove well this :

Lo, this is my suggestion ;
All things have due times,
Prayer, fasting, labour, all these ;
When time is not kept, that deed is ill ;
But more fully for your information,
Here is a man that liveth carefully,
Hath wife, children, and servants busy,
And other charges, that I not specify.
Is it lawful for this man
To leave his labour, used truly ?
His charges perish that God gave duly
And give him to prayer and ease of body ;
Whoso doth thus, with God is not then ;
Martha pleased God greatly thore.

    Mind. Yet Mary pleased him much the more.
    Lucifer. Yet the less had bliss for evermore,
Is that not enough ?
    Mind. Contemplative life is set before.
    Lucifer. I may not believe that in my lore ;
For God himself, when he was man born,
What life led he ? answer thou now !
Was he ever in contemplation ?
    Mind. I suppose not, by my relation.
    Lucifer. And all his life was information
And example to man.
Sometime with sinners he had conversation ;
Sometime with holy also communication ;
Sometime he laboured, prayed, sometime tribulation ;
That was *vita mixta* that God here began
And that life should ye here follow.
    Mind. I can believe what ye say is true.
    Lucifer. Contemplative life for to follow
It is great dread ; and see cause why :
They must fast, wake, and pray ever new,
Use hard living, and going with disciples due,
Keep silence, weep, and surfeits eschew.

                Vita mixta, A mixed life.

And if they fail of this they offend God highly.
When they have wasted by faintness
Then feeble their wits and fallen to dotage,
Sometimes into despair, and sometimes into madness.
Know it well, God is not pleased with this.
Leave, leave such singular business ;
Be in the world, use things necessary ;
The common is best, expressly ;
Who climbeth high his fall great is.

 Mind. Truly meseems you have reason.
 Lucifer. Apply you then to this conclusion.
 Mind. I can make no replication,
Your reasons be great ;
I cannot forget this information.
 Lucifer. Think thereupon is your salvation.
Now Understanding will have delectation
All singular devotions he would leave.
Your five wits abroad let spread ;
See how comely to man are precious clothes ;
What worship it is to be manful in deed
That bringeth in domination.
Of the simple what profits it to take heed ?
Behold how riches destroyeth need ;
It maketh man fair, him well for to feed.
Understanding tender ye this information.
 Understanding. In this I feel a manner of delectation.
 Lucifer. Ah, ha, sir ! then there make a pausation,
See and behold the world about ;
Little thing sufficeth to salvation,
All manner of sin destroyeth contrition,
They that despair mercy have great compunction,
God is pleased best with good will no doubt,
Therefore, Will, I rede you, incline
Leave your studies, though they be divine,
Your prayers, your penance, of hypocrisy the sign,
And lead a common life.
What sin is in meat, in ale, in wine ?
What sin is in riches, in clothing fine ?

Will. As the five wits give information
It seemeth your reasons be good.

Lucifer. The will of the soul hath free domination ;
Dispute not too much in this with reason ;
Yet the lower part to this taketh some instruction,
So should the other part, but he were mad.

Will. Meseem, as ye say, in body and soul
Man may be in the world, and be right good.

Lucifer. Yea, sir, by Saint Paul !
But trust not these preachers for they be not good,
For they flatter and lie, as they were mad ;
There is a wolf in a lambskin.

Will. Yea, I will no more row against the tide,
I will set my soul on a merry pin.

Lucifer. By my troth, that do ye wisely.
God loveth a clean soul and a merry,
Accord ye three together by
And ye may not miss fare.

Mind. To this suggestion agree I.

Understanding. Delight therein I have truly.

Will. I consent thereto freely.

Lucifer. Ah, ha, sirs ! all merry then, and away care.
Go in the world, see that about ;
Get good freely, cast no doubt ;
To the rich ye see men lowly bow,
Give to your body what is need
And ever be merry ; let revel rout !

Mind. Yea, else I beshrew my snout.

Understanding. And if I care, catch me the gout.

Will. And if I spare, the Devil me speed.

Lucifer. Go your way then and do wise
Change that sad array.   [*They go away.*
Then farewell, conscience he were numb
I should have all my will.
Reason I have made both deaf and dumb,
Thus by colours and false gin,
Many a soul from heaven I win !

                    [*Here he goeth his way, crying.*

Scene iv

Mind. Lo, me here in new array !
Whip, whip care away !
Farewell perfection !
    Understanding. All merry and glad now !
I have got goods, God wot how.
For joy I spring, I skip ;
Goods maketh one merry, to God avow.
Farewell, Conscience, I know not you !
I am at ease, had I enough ;
Truth, aside I let him slip.
    Will. Lo, here is one as jolly as you !
My heart is evermore light ;
I am full of felicity.
    Mind. And these be my single solace,
Kind fortune and grace,
Fortune in world's worship me doth involve,
Grace giveth curious eloquence, and that make
That all uncunning I disdain.
    Understanding. And my joy is especial
To hoard up riches, for fear to fall,
To see it, to handle it, to count it all,
And straitly to spare
To behold rich and royal
I boast, avaunt where I shall
Riches maketh a man equal
To them sometime his sovereigns were.
    Will. To me is joy most laudable
Speaking words delectable
Pertaining unto love ;
It is joy of joys inestimable.
    Mind. To avaunt thus, meseemeth it no shame,
For gallants now be in most fame ;
Courtly persons, men them proclaim,
Much we be set aside :
    Understanding. The rich covetous who dare blame,

Of usury and simony though he bear the name ?
To be false, men report it game,
It is called Wisdom.
   Will. These things be now so conversant,
We seem it no shame.
   Mind. Curious array will I ever haunt.
   Understanding. And I, falseness, to be passant.
   Will. And I, in lust my flesh to daunt ;
No man despise these ; they be but game.
   Mind. I rejoice of these ; now let us sing !
   Understanding. And if I spare evil joy, me wring.
   Will. Have at, quotha ! Lo, how I spring !
Lust maketh me wondrous wild.
   Mind. A tenor to you both I bring.
   Understanding. And I a mean for any king.
   Will. And but a treble I outwring.
The Devil him speed that mirth exiled.

                           [They sing.

   Mind. How be this, trow ye now ?
   Understanding. At the best, to God avow.
   Will. As merry as the bird on bough
I take no thought.
   Mind. The welfare of this world is in us, I avow.
   Understanding. Let each man tell his conditions
      how.
   Will. Begin ye, and have at you !
For I am ashamed of right nought.
   Mind. This is cause of my worship
I sue mighty lordship,
I am in great tendership
Therefore much folk me dread ;
Men sue to my friendship,
I support them by lordship.
   Understanding. And I use jurory,
Embrace guests of perjury,
Chop and change with simony,
And take large gifts ;
Be the case never so true
(2,753)

                                15

I prove it false, I swear, I lie ;
With a guest of mine affy
The ready way this now to thrift is.

Will. What trow ye, by me.
More than I take spend I thrice three ;
Sometime I give, sometime they me,
And I am ever fresh and gay.

Mind. Law proceedeth not for maintenance.

Understanding. Truth recurreth not for abundance.

Will. And lust is in so great usance
We heed it nought.

Mind. In us the world hath most affiance.

Understanding. None there be in so great acquaintance.

Will. Few there be out of our alliance,
While the world is thus we take no thought.

Mind. Thought ! nay, there against strive I.

Understanding. Who will have law, must have
money.

Will. There poverty is the poor wretch,
Though right he be, he shall never attain.

Mind. Wrong is borne up boldly,
Though all the world know it openly,
Maintenance is not so mighty,
All is all for meed.

Understanding. The law is so coloured falsely,
By sleights and by perjury,
Bribes be so greedy
That to the poor truth is taken no heed.

Will. Maintenance and perjury now stand,
That were never so much regnant
Since Christ was born.

Understanding. So we three be now in hand.

Will. Yea, and welcomed everywhere.

Maintenance, An evil custom of the fifteenth century, by which
lords attended courts of justice with armed men at their back
to ensure a sentence in their favour.
Meed, Bribery.

Mind. Now we three do make a dance,
And those that belong to our retinaunce
Coming in be countenance,
This were a disport.

[*Disguised figures, servants and abettors of Mind, Will,
and Understanding, now enter ; and a general dance
concludes the play.*

CHAPTER XX.—EVERYMAN

OUR last play dates from the end of the fifteenth
century, when the Middle Ages had all but given way
before the new ideas of the modern world. This play,
however, belongs essentially to the Middle Ages, for it
is *Everyman*, one of the greatest of English morality
plays. It tells how Everyman, called upon by Death
to make his last pilgrimage, asks of his friends who
will accompany him. All of them, Beauty, Strength,
Discretion, and the rest, forsake him, save only Good-
Deeds and Knowledge, who endure with him to the
end. With this play we must leave our study of the
plays of the Middle Ages, for the morality was the last
form of the drama which we can definitely associate
with that period of history. With the plays of the
sixteenth century we are in the century of Shakespeare,
and we begin to meet with the first plays of the modern
world.

Everyman.

*Here beginneth a treatise how the High Father of Heaven
sendeth Death to summon every creature to come
and give account of their lives in this world, and is
in manner of a moral play.*

Enter a Messenger, as Prologue.

Messenger. I pray you all give your audience,
And hear this matter with reverence,

By figure a moral play—
The *Summoning of Everyman* called it is,
That of our lives and ending shows
How transitory we be all day.
The story saith,—Man, in the beginning,
Look well, and take good heed to the ending,
Be you never so gay !
Ye think sin in the beginning full sweet,
Which in the end causeth thy soul to weep,
When the body lieth in clay.
Here shall you see how *Fellowship* and *Jollity*,
Both *Strength*, *Pleasure*, and *Beauty*,
Will fade from thee as flower in May.
For ye shall hear, how our heaven king
Calleth *Everyman* to a general reckoning :
Give audience, and hear what he doth say.

                                        [*Exit Messenger.*

God speaketh.

   God. I perceive here in my majesty,
How that all creatures be to me unkind,
Living without dread in worldly prosperity :
Of ghostly sight the people be so blind,
Drowned in sin, they know me not for their God ;
In worldly riches is all their mind,
They fear not my righteousness, that sharp rod ;
My law that I shewed, when I for them died,
They forget clean, and shedding of my blood red ;
Everyman liveth so after his own pleasure,
And yet of their life they be nothing sure :
Therefore I will in all the haste
Have a reckoning of Everyman's person.
For and I leave the people thus alone
In their life and wicked tempests,
Verily they will become much worse than beasts ;

For now one would by envy another up eat;
Charity they all do clean forget.
I hoped well that Everyman
In my glory should make his mansion,
And thereto I had them all elect;
But now I see, like traitors deject,
They thank me not for the pleasure that I to them
    meant,
Nor yet for their being that I them have lent;
I proffered the people great multitude of mercy,
And few there be that asketh it heartily;
They be so cumbered with worldly riches,
That needs on them I must do justice,
On Everyman living without fear.
Where art thou, *Death*, thou mighty messenger?

Enter Death.

   Death. Almighty God, I am here at your will,
Your commandment to fulfil.
   God. Go thou to *Everyman*,
And show him in my name
A pilgrimage he must on him take,
Which he in no wise may escape;
And that he bring with him a sure reckoning
Without delay or any tarrying.
   Death. Lord, I will in the world go run over all,
And truly outsearch both great and small;
Everyman will I beset that liveth beastly
Out of God's laws, and dreadeth not folly:
He that loveth riches I will strike with my dart,
His sight to blind, and from heaven depart,
Except that alms be his good friend,
In hell for to dwell, world without end.
Lo, yonder I see *Everyman* walking;
Full little he thinketh on my coming;
His mind is on fleshly lusts and his treasure,
And great pain it shall cause him to endure
Before the Lord Heaven King.   [*Enter Everyman.*

Everyman, stand still ; whither art thou going
Thus gaily ?   Hast thou thy Maker forgot ?
    Everyman. Why askest thou ?
Wouldest thou know ?
    Death. Yea, sir, I will show you ;
In great haste I am sent to thee
From God out of his majesty.
    Everyman. What, sent to me ?
    Death. Yea, certainly.
Though thou have forgot him here,
He thinketh on thee in the heavenly sphere,
As, or we depart, thou shalt know.
    Everyman. What desireth God of me ?
                    Death. That shall I show thee ;
                    A reckoning he will needs have
                    Without any longer respite.
                        Everyman. To give a reckoning longer
                            leisure I crave ;
                    This blind matter troubleth my wit.
                        Death. On thee thou must take a
                            long journey :
                    Therefore thy book of count with thee
                            thou bring ;
                    For turn again thou can not by no
                            way,

Everyman.

And look thou be sure of thy reckoning :
For before God shalt thou answer, and show
Thy many bad deeds and good but a few ;
How thou hast spent thy life, and in what wise,
Before the chief lord of paradise.
    Everyman. Full unready I am such reckoning to give.
I know thee not : what messenger art thou ?
    Death. I am *Death*, that no man dreadeth.
For every man I rest and none spareth ;
For it is God's commandment
That all to me should be obedient.
    Everyman. O *Death*, thou comest when I had thee
            least in mind ;

In thy power it lieth me to save,
Yet of my good will I give thee, if ye will be kind,
Yea, a thousand pound shalt thou have,
And defer this matter till another day.

Death. *Everyman*, it may not be by no way ;
I set not by gold, silver, nor riches,
Ne by pope, emperor, king, duke, ne princes.
For and I would receive gifts great,
All the world I might get ;
But my custom is clean contrary.
I give thee no respite : come hence, and not tarry.

Everyman. O gracious God, in the high seat celestial,
Have mercy on me in this most need ;
Shall I have no company from this vale terrestrial
Of mine acquaintance that way me to lead ?

Death. Yea, if any be so hardy,
That would go with thee and bear thee company.
Hie thee that thou were gone to God's magnificence,
Thy reckoning to give before his presence.
What, weenest thou thy life is given thee,
And thy worldly goods also ?

Everyman. I had thought so, verily.

Death. Nay, nay ; it was but lent thee ;
For as soon as thou art gone,
Another awhile shall have it, and then go therefro
Even as thou hast done.
Everyman, thou art mad ; thou hast thy wits five,
And here on earth will not amend thy life,
For suddenly I do come.

Everyman. O wretched caitiff, whither shall I flee,
That I might scape this endless sorrow !
Now, gentle *Death*, spare me till to-morrow,
That I may amend me
With good advisement.

Death. Nay, thereto I will not consent,
Nor no man will I respite,
But to the heart suddenly I shall smite
Without any advisement.

And now out of sight I will me hie;
See thou make thee ready shortly,
For thou mayst say this is the day
That no man living may scape away.

[*Exit Death.*

   Everyman. Alas, I may well weep with sighs deep;
Now have I no manner of company
To help me in my journey, and me to keep;
And also my writing is full unready.
How shall I do now for to excuse me?
I would to God I had never been born!
To my soul a full great profit it had be;
For now I fear pains huge and great.
The time passeth; Lord, help that all wrought;
For though I mourn it availeth nought.
The day passeth, and is almost a-go;
I wot not well what for to do.
To whom were I best my complaint to make?
What, and I to *Fellowship* thereof spake,
And showed him of this sudden chance?
For in him is all mine affiance;
We have in the world so many a day
Been good friends in sport and play.
I see him yonder, certainly;
I trust that he will bear me company;
Therefore to him will I speak to ease my sorrow.

[*Enter Fellowship.*

Well met, good *Fellowship*, and good morrow!
   Fellowship. Everyman, good morrow by this day.
Sir, why lookest thou so piteously?
If any thing be amiss, I pray thee, me say,
That I may help to remedy.
   Everyman. Yea, good *Fellowship*, yea,
I am in great jeopardy.
   Fellowship. My true friend, show to me your mind
I will not forsake thee, unto my life's end,
In the way of good company.
   Everyman. That is well spoken, and lovingly.

Fellowship. Sir, I must needs know your heaviness ;
I have pity to see you in any distress ;
If any have you wronged ye shall revenged be,
Though I on the ground be slain for thee,—
Though that I know before that I should die.

    Everyman. Verily, *Fellowship*, gramercy.

    Fellowship. Tush ! by thy thanks I set not a straw.
Show me your grief, and say no more.

    Everyman. Then be you a good friend at need :
I have found you true here before.

    Fellowship. And so ye shall evermore ;
For, in faith, and thou go to Hell,
I will not forsake thee by the way !

    Everyman. Ye speak like a good friend ; I believe
        you well ;
I shall deserve it, and I may.

    Fellowship. I speak of no deserving, by this day.
For he that will say and nothing do
Is not worthy with good company to go ;
Therefore show me the grief of your mind,
As to your friend most loving and kind.

    Everyman. I shall show you how it is ;
Commanded I am to go a journey,
A long way, hard and dangerous,
And give a strait count without delay
Before the high judge Adonai.
Wherefore I pray you, bear me company,
As ye have promised, in this journey.

    Fellowship. That is matter indeed ! Promise is
        duty,
But, and I should take such a voyage on me,
I know it well, it should be to my pain :
Also it maketh me afeard, certain.
But let us take counsel here as well as we can,
For your words would fear a strong man.

    Everyman. Why, ye said, If I had need,

Adonai, God.

Ye would me never forsake, quick nor dead,
Though it were to hell truly.

Fellowship. So I said, certainly,
But such pleasures be set aside, the sooth to say :
And also, if we took such a journey,
When should we come again ?

Everyman. Nay, never again till the day of doom.

Fellowship. In faith, then will not I come there !
Who hath you these tidings brought ?

Everyman. Indeed, *Death* was with me here.

Fellowship. Now, by God that all hath bought,
If *Death* were the messenger,
For no man that is living to-day
I will not go that loathsome journey—

Everyman. Gentle *fellow*, help me in my necessity ;
We have loved long, and now I need,
And now, gentle *Fellowship*, remember me.

Fellowship. Whether ye have loved me or no,
By Saint John, I will not with thee go.

Everyman. Yet I pray thee, take the labour, and do
    so much for me
To bring me forward, for saint charity,
And comfort me till I come without the town.

Fellowship. Nay, and thou would give me a new
    gown,
I will not one foot with thee go ;
But and thou had tarried I would not have left thee so.
And as now, God speed thee in thy journey,
For from thee I will depart as fast as I may.

Everyman. Whither away, *Fellowship ?* Wilt thou
    forsake me ?

Fellowship. Yea, by my fay, to God I betake thee.

Everyman. Farewell, good *Fellowship ;* for thee my
    heart is sore.

Fellowship. Adieu, for ever, I shall see thee no more.
In faith, *Everyman,* farewell now at the end ;
For you I will remember that parting is mourning.
                                        [*Exit Fellowship.*

Everyman. Lo, *Fellowship* forsaketh me in my most
  need :
For help in this world whither shall I resort ?
Fellowship herebefore with me would merry make ·
And now little sorrow for me doth he take.
It is said, in prosperity men friends may find,
Which in adversity be full unkind.
Now whither for succour shall I flee,
Sith that *Fellowship* hath forsaken me ?
To my kinsmen I will truly,
Praying them to help me in my necessity ;
I believe that they will do so.
I will go say, for yonder I see them go,
Where be ye now, my friends and kinsmen ?

Enter Kindred and Cousin.

Kindred. Here be we now at your commandment.
Cousin, I pray you show us your intent
In any wise, and do not spare.
Cousin. Yea, *Everyman,* and to us declare
If ye be disposed to go any whither,
For wot ye well, we will live and die together.
Kindred. In wealth and woe we will with you hold,
For over his kin a man may be bold.
Everyman. Gramercy, my friends and kinsmen kind.
Now shall I show you the grief of my mind :
I was commanded by a messenger,
That is an high king's chief officer ;
He bade me go a pilgrimage to my pain,
And I know well I shall never come again ;
Also I must give reckoning straight,
For I have a great enemy, that hath me in wait,
Which intendeth me for to hinder.
Kindred. What account is that which ye must
  render ?
That would I know.
Everyman. Of all my works I must show
How I have lived and my days spent ;

Also of ill deeds, that I have used
In my time, sith life was me lent ;
And of all virtues that I have refused.
Therefore I pray you go thither with me,
To help to make mine account, for saint charity.

 Cousin. What, to go thither ? Is that the matter ?
Nay, *Everyman*, I had liefer fast bread and water
All this five year and more.

 Everyman. Alas, that ever I was born !
For now shall I never be merry
If that you forsake me.

 Kindred. Ah, sir ; what, ye be a merry man !
Take good heart to you, and make no moan.
But one thing I warn you, by Saint Anne,
As for me, ye shall go alone.

 Everyman. My *Cousin*, will you not with me go ?
 Cousin. No, by our Lady ; I have the cramp in my toe.
Trust not to me, for, so God me speed,
I will deceive you in your most need.

 Everyman. Now show me the very effect of your mind.
Will you go with me, or abide behind ?

 Kindred. Abide behind ? yea, that I will and I may !
Therefore farewell until another day.

         [Exit Kindred.

 Everyman. How should I be merry or glad ?
For fair promises men to me do make,
But when I have most need, they me forsake.
I am deceived ; that maketh me sad.

 Cousin. Cousin *Everyman*, farewell now,
For verily I will not go with you ;
Also of mine own an unready reckoning
I have to account ; therefore I make tarrying
Now, God keep thee, for now I go.

         [Exit Cousin.

Everyman. Ah, *Jesus,* is all come hereto ?
Lo, fair words maketh fools feign ;
They promise and nothing will do certain.
My kinsmen promised me faithfully
For to abide with me steadfastly,
And now fast away do they flee :
Even so *Fellowship* promised me.
What friend were best me help to provide ?
I lose my time here longer to abide.
Yet in my mind a thing there is ;—
All my life I have loved riches ;
If that my good now help me might,
He would make my heart full light.
I will speak to him in this distress.—
Where art thou, my *Goods* and riches ?

Enter Goods.

Goods. Who calleth me ? *Everyman ?* what haste
    thou hast !
I lie here in corners, trussed and piled so high,
And in chests I am locked full fast,
Also sacked in bags, thou mayst see with thine eye,
I cannot stir ; in packs low I lie.
What would ye have, lightly me say.
    Everyman. Come hither, *Goods,* in all the haste thou
        may,
For of counsel I must desire thee.
    Goods. Sir, and ye in the world have trouble or
        adversity,
That can I help you to remedy shortly.
    Everyman. It is another disease that grieveth me ;
In this world it is not, I tell thee so.
I am sent for another way to go,
To give a straight account general
Before the highest *Jupiter* of all ;
And all my life I have had joy and pleasure in thee,
Therefore I pray thee go with me,
For, peradventure, thou mayst before God Almighty

My reckoning help to clean and purify ;
For it is said ever among,
That money maketh all right that is wrong.

    Goods. Nay, *Everyman,* I sing another song,
I follow no man in such voyages :
For and I went with thee
Thou shouldst fare much the worse for me ;
For because on me thou did set thy mind,
Thy reckoning I have made blotted and blind,
That thine account thou cannot make truly ;
And that hast thou for the love of me.

    Everyman. That would grieve me full sore,
When I should come to that fearful answer.
Up, let us go thither together.

    Goods. Nay, not so, I am too brittle, I may not
        endure ;
I will follow no man one foot, be thou sure.

    Everyman. Alas, I have thee loved, and had great
        pleasure
All my life-days on goods and treasure.

    Goods. That is to thy damnation without lesing,
For my love is contrary to the love everlasting.
But if thou had me loved moderately during,
As, to the poor to give part of me,
Then shouldst thou not in this dolour be,
Nor in this great sorrow and care.
A season thou hast had me in prosperity ;
My condition is man's soul to kill ;
If I save one, a thousand I do spill ;
Weenest thou that I will follow thee ?
From this world, nay, verily.

    Everyman. I had thought otherwise.

    Goods. Therefore to thy soul *Good* is a thief ;
For when thou art dead, this is my guise
Another to deceive in the same wise
As I have done thee, and all to his soul's reprief.

    Everyman. O false *Good,* cursed thou be !
Thou traitor to God, that hast deceived me,

And caught me in thy snare.

   Goods. Marry, thou brought thyself in care,
Whereof I am glad,
I must needs laugh, I cannot be sad.

   Everyman. Ah, *Good*, thou hast had long my
           heartly love ;
I gave thee that which should be the Lord's above.
But wilt thou not go with me indeed ?
I pray thee truth to say.

   Goods. No, so God me speed,
Therefore farewell, and have good day.

                        [Exit Goods.

   Everyman. O, to whom shall I make my moan
For to go with me in that heavy journey ?
First *Fellowship*, he said he would with me go ;
His words were very pleasant and gay,
But afterward he left me alone.
Then spake I to my kinsmen all in despair,
And also they gave me words fair,
They lacked no fair speaking,
But all forsake me in the ending.
Then went I to my *Goods* that I loved best,
In hope to have comfort, but there had I least ;
For my *Goods* sharply did me tell
That he bringeth many into hell.
Then of myself I was ashamed,
And so I am worthy to be blamed ;
Thus may I well myself hate.
Of whom shall I now counsel take ?
I think that I shall never speed
Till that I go to my *Good-Deed,*
But alas, she is so weak,
That she can neither go nor speak ;
Yet will I venture on her now.—
My *Good-Deeds*, where be you ?

   Enter Good-Deeds.   *She falls to the ground.*

   Good-Deeds. Here I lie cold in the ground ;

Thy sins have me sore bound,
That I cannot stir.

    Everyman. O, *Good-Deeds*, I stand in fear ;
I must you pray of counsel,
For help now should come right well.

    Good-Deeds. Everyman, I have understanding
That thou art summoned account to make
Before *Messias*, of Jerusalem King.

    Everyman. Therefore I come to you, my moan to
        make ;
I pray thee to go with me.

    Good-Deeds. I would full fain, but I cannot stand
        verily.

    Everyman. Good-Deeds, I pray you, help me in this
        need,
Or else I am for ever damned indeed ;
Therefore help me to make my reckoning
Before the redeemer of all thing,
That king is, and was, and ever shall.

    Good-Deeds. Everyman, I am sorry of your fall,
And fain would I help you, and I were able.

    Everyman. Good-Deeds, your counsel I pray you
        give me.

    Good-Deeds. That shall I do verily ;
Though that on my feet I may not go,
I have a sister, that shall with you also,
Called *Knowledge*, which shall with you abide,
To help you to make that dreadful reckoning.

Enter Knowledge.

    Knowledge. Everyman, I will go with thee, and be
        thy guide,
In thy most need to go by thy side.

    Everyman. In good condition I am now in every
        thing,
And am wholly content with this good thing ;
Thanked be God my Creator.

    Good-Deeds. And when he hath brought thee there,

Where thou shalt heal thee of thy smart,
Then go you with your reckoning and your *Good-Deeds*
      together
For to make thee joyful at heart
Before the blessed Trinity.

    Everyman. My *Good-Deeds*, I thank thee heartfully:
I am well content, certainly,
With your words sweet.

    <u>*Knowledge.*</u> Now go we thither lovingly,
To *Confession*, that cleansing river.

    Everyman. For joy I weep ; I would we were there ;
But, I pray you to instruct me by intellection
Where dwelleth that holy man, *Confession.*

    Knowledge. In the house of salvation :
We shall find him in that place,
That shall us comfort by God's grace.

                   [Exit Knowledge and Everyman.

Enter Knowledge and Everyman, meeting Confession.

    Knowledge. Lo, this is *Confession ;* kneel down and
      ask mercy,
For he is in good conceit with God almighty.

    Everyman. O glorious fountain that all uncleanness
      doth clarify,
Wash from me the spots of vices unclean,
That on me no sin may be seen ;
I come with *Knowledge* for my redemption,
Redeemed with heart and full of contrition ;
For I am commanded a pilgrimage to take,
And great accounts before God to make.
Now, I pray you, *Shrift,* mother of salvation,
Help my good deeds for my piteous exclamation.

    Confession. I know your sorrow well, *Everyman ;*
Because with *Knowledge* ye come to me,
I will you comfort as well as I can,

(2,753)   16

And a precious jewel I will give thee,
Called penance, wise voider of adversity ;
Therewith shall your body chastised be,
With abstinence and perseverance in God's service :
Here shall you receive that scourge of me,
Which is penance strong, that ye must endure,
To remember thy Saviour was scourged for thee
With sharp scourges, and suffered it patiently ;
So must thou, or thou scape that painful pilgrimage ;
Knowledge, keep him in this voyage,
And by that time *Good-Deeds* will be with thee.
But in any wise, be sure of mercy,
For your time draweth fast, and ye will saved be ;
Ask God mercy, and He will grant truly,
When with the scourge of penance man doth him bind,
The oil of forgiveness then shall he find.

[Exit Confession.

Everyman. Thanked be God for his gracious work !
For now I will my penance begin ;
This hath rejoiced and lighted my heart,
Though the knots be painful and hard within.

   Knowledge. Everyman, your penance look that ye
     fulfil,
What pain that ever it to you be,
And *Knowledge* will give you counsel at will,
How your accounts ye shall make clearly.

   Everyman. O blessed Godhead, elect and high-
     divine,
Forgive me my grievous offence ;
Here I cry thee mercy in this presence.
O ghostly treasure, O ransomer and redeemer
Of all the world, hope and conductor,
Mirror of joy, and founder of mercy,
Which illumineth heaven and earth thereby,
Hear my clamorous complaint, though it late be ;
Receive my prayers of thy benignity ;
Though I be a sinner most abominable,
Yet let my name be written in *Moses'* table ;

Knowledge, give me the scourge of penance ;
My flesh therewith shall give a quittance :
I will now begin, if God give me grace.

   Knowledge. Everyman, God give you time and
      space :
Thus I bequeath you in the hands of our Saviour,
Thus may you make your reckoning sure.

   Everyman. In the name of the Holy Trinity,
My body sore punished shall be :
Take this body for the sin of the flesh ;
Also thou delightest to go gay and fresh,
And in way of damnation thou did me bring ;
Therefore suffer now strokes and punishing.
Now of penance I will wade the water clear,
To save me from purgatory, that sharp fire.

   [*During this speech Everyman flogs himself with
     the whip which he received from Confession.*

          Enter Good-Deeds, walking.

   Good-Deeds. I thank God, now I can walk and go ;
And am delivered of my sickness and woe.
Therefore with *Everyman* I will go, and not spare ;
His good works I will help him to declare.

   Knowledge. Now, *Everyman,* be merry and glad ;
Your *Good-Deeds* do come ; ye may not be sad ;
Now is your *Good-Deeds* whole and sound,
Going upright upon the ground.

   Everyman. My heart is light, and shall be evermore ;
Now will I smite faster than I did before.

   Good-Deeds. Everyman, pilgrim, my special friend,
Blessed be thou without end ;
For thee is prepared the eternal glory.

   Everyman. Welcome, my *Good-Deeds ;* now I hear
     thy voice,
I weep for very sweetness of love.

   Knowledge. Be no more sad, but evermore rejoice,
God seeth thy living in his throne above ;
Put on this garment to thy behove,

Which with your tears is now all wet ;
Lest before God it be unsweet,
When you to your journey's end come shall.

> [*Everyman puts on a garment which is given to him by Knowledge.*

Everyman. Gentle *Knowledge*, what do you it call ?

Knowledge. It is the garment of sorrow :
From pain it will you borrow ;
Contrition it is,
That getteth forgiveness ;
It pleaseth God passing well.

Everyman. Now blessed be *Jesu, Mary's* Son !
For now have I on true contrition.
And let us go now without tarrying ;
Good-Deeds, have we clear our reckoning ?

Good-Deeds. Yea, indeed I have it here.

Everyman. Then I trust we need not fear ;
Now, friends, let us not part in twain.

Knowledge. Nay, *Everyman*, that will we not, certain.

Good-Deeds. Yet must thou lead with thee
Three persons of great might.

Everyman. Who should they be ?

Good-Deeds. *Discretion* and *Strength* they hight,
And thy *Beauty* may not abide behind.

Knowledge. Also ye must call to mind
Your *Five-wits* as for your counsellors.

Good-Deeds. You must have them ready at all hours.

Everyman. How shall I get them hither ?

Knowledge. You must call them all together,
And they will hear you incontinent.

Everyman. My friends, come hither and be present,
Discretion, Strength, my *Five-wits*, and *Beauty*.

> *Enter Discretion, Strength, Five-wits, and Beauty.*

Beauty. Here at your will we be all ready.
What will ye that we should do ?

Good-Deeds. That ye would with *Everyman* go,

And help him in his pilgrimage,
Advise you, will ye with him or not in that voyage ?
   Strength. We will bring him all thither,
To his help and comfort, ye may believe me.
   Discretion. So will we go with him all together.
   Everyman. Almighty God, loved may thou be,
I give thee laud that I have hither brought
Strength, Discretion, Beauty, and *Five-wits ;* lack I
      nought ;
And my *Good-Deeds,* with *Knowledge* clear,
All be in company at my will here ;
I desire no more to my business.
   Strength. And I, *Strength,* will stand by you in
      distress,
Though thou wouldst in battle fight on the ground.
   Five-wits. And though it were through the world
      round,
We will not depart for sweet nor sour.
   Beauty. No more will I unto death's hour,
Whatsoever thereof befall.
   Discretion. Everyman, advise you first of all ;
Go with a good advisement and deliberation ;
We all give you virtuous monition
That all shall be well.
   Everyman. My friends, hearken what I will tell :
I pray God reward you in his heavenly sphere.
Now hearken, all that be here,
For I will make my testament
Here before you all present.
In alms half my good I will give with my hands twain
In the way of charity, with good intent,
And the other half still shall remain
In quiet to be returned where it ought to be.
This I do in despite of the fiend of hell
To go quite out of his peril
Ever after and this day.
   Knowledge. Everyman, hearken what I say ;
Go to priesthood, I you advise,

And receive of him in any wise
The holy sacrament and ointment together ;
Then shortly see ye turn again hither ;
We will all abide you here.

    Five-wits. Yea, *Everyman,* hie you that ye ready
         were,
There is no emperor, king, duke, ne baron,
That of God hath commission,
As hath the least priest in the world being ;
For of the blessed sacraments pure and benign,
He beareth the keys and thereof hath he cure
For man's redemption, it is ever sure.

    Everyman. Fain would I receive that holy body
And meekly to my ghostly father I will go.

    Five-wits. Everyman, that is the best that ye can do :
God will you to salvation bring.

                  [Exit Everyman in search of a priest.
    (*To Knowledge*). No remedy we find under God
But all only priesthood.
God gave priests that dignity,
And setteth them in his stead among us to be ;
Thus be they above angels in degree.

    Knowledge. If priests be good it is so surely ;
Sinful priests giveth the sinners example bad.

    Five-wits. I trust to God no such may we find ;
Therefore let us priesthood honour,
And follow their doctrine for our souls' succour ;
We be their sheep, and they shepherds be
By whom we all be kept in surety.
Peace, for yonder I see *Everyman* come,
Which hath made true satisfaction.

    Good-Deeds. Methinketh it is he indeed.

            Re-enter Everyman.

    Everyman. Now Jesu Christ be your alder speed.
I have received the sacrament for my redemption,

        Alder speed, Speed in help of all.

And then mine extreme unction :
Blessed be all they that counselled me to take it !
And now, friends, let us go without longer respite ;
I thank God that ye have tarried so long.
Now set each of you on this rod your hand,
And shortly follow me :
I go before, there I would be ; God be our guide.
 Strength. *Everyman*, we will not from you go,
Till ye have gone this voyage long.
 Discretion. I, *Discretion*, will bide by you also.
 Knowledge. And though this pilgrimage be never so
   strong,
I will never part you fro :
Everyman, I will be as sure by thee
As ever I did by Judas Maccabee.
 Everyman. Alas, I am so faint I may not stand,
My limbs under me do fold ;
Friends, let us not turn again to this land,
Not for all the world's gold,
     [*Here Everyman comes to his grave.*
For into this cave must I creep
And turn to the earth and there to sleep.
 Beauty. What, into this grave ? alas !
 Everyman. Yea, there shall you consume more and
   less.
 Beauty. And what, should I smother here ?
 Everyman. Yea, by my faith, and never more
   appear.
In this world live no more we shall,
But in heaven before the highest Lord of all.
 Beauty. I cross out all this ; adieu by Saint *John ;*
I take my cap in my lap and am gone.
 Everyman. What, *Beauty*, whither will ye ?
 Beauty. Peace, I am deaf ; I look not behind me,
Not and thou would give me all the gold in thy chest.
        [*Exit Beauty.*
 Everyman. Alas, whereto may I trust ?
Beauty goeth fast away from me ;

She promised with me to live and die.

    Strength. Everyman, I will thee also forsake and
        deny ;

Thy game liketh me not at all.

    Everyman. Why, then ye will forsake me all.

Sweet *Strength*, tarry a little space.

    Strength. Nay, sir, by the rood of grace

I will hie me from thee fast,

Though thou weep till thy heart brast.

    Everyman. Ye would ever bide by me, ye said.

    Strength. Yea, I have you far enough conveyed ;

Ye be old enough, I understand,

Your pilgrimage to take on hand ;

I repent me that I hither came.

    Everyman. Strength, you to displease I am to blame ;

Will you break promise that is debt ?

    Strength. In faith, I care not ;

Thou art but a fool to complain,

You spend your speech and waste your brain ;

Go thrust thee into the ground.

                         [Exit Strength.

    Everyman. I had thought surer I should you have
        found.

He that trusteth in his *Strength*

She him deceiveth at the length.

Both *Strength* and *Beauty* forsaketh me,

Yet they promised me fair and lovingly.

    Discretion. Everyman, I will after *Strength* be gone ;

As for me, I will leave you alone.

    Everyman. Why, *Discretion*, will ye forsake me ?

    Discretion. Yea, in faith, I will go from thee,

For when *Strength* goeth before

I follow after evermore.

    Everyman. Yet, I pray thee, for the love of the
        Trinity,

Look in my grave once piteously.

    Discretion. Nay, so nigh will I not come.

Farewell, every one !   *[Exit Discretion.*

Everyman. O all thing faileth, save God alone ;
Beauty, Strength, and *Discretion ;*
For when *Death* bloweth his blast,
They all run from me full fast.

Five-wits. Everyman, of thee now my leave I take ;
I will follow the other, for here I thee forsake.

Everyman. Alas ! then may I wail and weep,
For I took you for my best friend.

Five-wits. I will no longer thee keep ;
Now farewell, and there an end.

[*Exit Five-wits.*

Everyman. O Jesu, help, all hath forsaken me !

Good-Deeds. Nay, *Everyman,* I will bide with thee,
I will not forsake thee indeed ;
Thou shalt find me a good friend at need.

Everyman. Gramercy, *Good-Deeds ;* now may I true
friends see ;
They have forsaken me every one ;
I loved them better than my *Good-Deeds* alone.
Knowledge, will ye forsake me also ?

Knowledge. Yea, *Everyman,* when ye to death do go :
But not yet for no manner of danger.

Everyman. Gramercy, *Knowledge,* with all my heart.

Knowledge. Nay, yet I will not from hence depart,
Till I see where ye shall be come.

Everyman. Methinketh, alas, that I must be gone,
To make my reckoning and my debts pay,
For I see my time is nigh spent away.
Take example, all ye that this do hear or see,
How they that I loved best do forsake me,
Except my *Good-Deeds* that bideth truly.

Good-Deeds. All earthly thing is but vanity :
Beauty, Strength, and *Discretion* do man forsake,
Foolish friends and kinsmen, that fair spake,
All fleeth save *Good-Deeds,* and that am I.

Everyman. Have mercy on me, God most mighty ;
And stand by me, thou Mother and Maid, holy *Mary.*

Good-Deeds. Fear not, I will speak for thee.

Everyman. Here I cry God mercy.

Good-Deeds. Short our end, and minish our pain ;
Let us go and never come again.

Everyman. Into thy hands, Lord, my soul I com-
mend ;
Receive it, Lord, that it be not lost ;
As thou me boughtest, so me defend,
And save me from the fiend's boast,
That I may appear with that blessed host
That shall be saved at the day of doom.
In manus tuas—of might's most
For ever—*commendo spiritum meum.*

> [*Everyman sinks into his grave.*

Knowledge. Now hath he suffered that we all shall
endure ;
The *Good-Deeds* shall make all sure.
Now hath he made ending ;
Methinketh that I hear angels sing
And make great joy and melody,
Where *Everyman's* soul shall received be.

Enter an Angel who raises Everyman from his grave.

Angel. Come, excellent elect spouse to Jesu :
Hereabove thou shalt go
Because of thy singular virtue :
Now thy soul is taken thy body fro ;
Thy reckoning is crystal-clear.
Now shalt thou into the heavenly sphere,
Unto the which all ye shall come
That liveth well, before the day of doom.

> [*The Angel leads away Everyman, Good-Deeds,
> and Knowledge.*

Enter a Doctor for the Epilogue.

Doctor. This memorial men may have in mind ;
Ye hearers, take it of worth, old and young,

In manus . . . meum, "Into thy hands I commend my soul."

And forsake pride, for he deceiveth you in the end,
And remember *Beauty*, *Five-wits*, *Strength*, and
            Discretion,
They all at the last do *Everyman* forsake,
Save his *Good-Deeds*, there doth he take.
But beware, for and they be small
Before God, he hath no help at all.
None excuse may be there for *Everyman* :
Alas, how shall he do then ?
For after death amends may no man make,
For then mercy and pity do him forsake.
If his reckoning be not clear when he do come,
God will say—*ite maledicti in ignem æternum.*
And he that hath his account whole and sound,
High in heaven he shall be crowned ;
Unto which place God bring us all thither
That we may live body and soul together.
Thereto help the Trinity,
Amen, say ye, for saint *Charity*.

THUS ENDETH THIS MORAL PLAY OF EVERYMAN.

Ite . . . æternum, " Go, ye accursed ones, into eternal fire."

THE END

PATTERN PLAYS

A Book of Plays and Play-Making

By E. C. OAKDEN and
MARY STURT

---

176 pages.

With Frontispiece showing a Seventeenth-century Playhouse

¶ The object of this Book is to interest Middle Form pupils in the craftsmanship of plays by showing how stories can be converted into dramas.

¶ The Volume is therefore not only a reading-book which prompts pupils to do things, but also a manual of composition of a distinctly novel kind.

¶ The method of the Authors is to show how a story or poem can be turned into a play and then to provide similar stories for the pupil's own use.

¶ An interesting Introduction deals with the Unities of Time, Place, and Action, and with the art of Stage Direction.

¶ The stories dealt with are : *The Pied Piper ; King John and the Abbot of Canterbury ; The Travelling Musicians* (Grimm); *Pastorella* (from *The Faerie Queene*); *Robin Hood and Alan-a-Dale ; The Luck of Troy* (Homer); *The Story of Dorigen* (Chaucer) ; *The Tale of Griselda* (Chaucer) ; *Twice is Too Much (Arabian Nights) ; Caliph for a Day (Arabian Nights) ; The Swineherd* (Andersen) ; *The Emperor's New Clothes* (Andersen) ; *Lady Clare* (Tennyson) ; *The Jackdaw of Rheims.*

¶ The Appendix contains further help for teachers and older students.

THOMAS NELSON AND SONS, LTD.

SHAKESPEARE'S
RICHARD THE SECOND

Edited by HENRY NEWBOLT

"The reader acts the play himself
in the theatre of his own mind."

***

176 pages. Illustrated.

With Frontispiece Portrait of Richard II

***

¶ The appearance of yet another School Shakespeare demands justification, if not an apology.

¶ This Edition is intended for those teachers who consider that the dramatic side of the poet's genius has recently been over-emphasized; who remember that Shakespeare was a poet as well as a dramatist, and that his most intimate and lasting appeal is to the mind and the emotions, rather than to the eye and ear.

¶ The keynote of the new Edition is contained in the words printed above in heavy type and drawn from Sir Henry Newbolt's General Introduction.

¶ The Glossary takes the form of footnotes; the Illustrated Introduction gives enough information to help the reader to visualize the period ; the well-printed Text is followed by a Commentary dealing *seriatim* with all the questions raised by the play—historical, literary, dramatic.

¶ While this Edition can be keenly enjoyed as a literary masterpiece, it contains all the information necessary for pupils taking the play for a modern examination. Moreover, the dramatic aspect, though subordinated to the imaginative, is not neglected.

***

THOMAS NELSON AND SONS, Ltd.

SHAKESPEARE'S

A MIDSUMMER
NIGHT'S DREAM

Edited by EVELYN SMITH, B.A.

"The reader acts the play himself
in the theatre of his own mind."

128 pages.   Illustrated.

With Frontispiece of Puck by E. Heber Thompson

¶ The Editor has modelled this Edition upon the
Richard II of Sir Henry Newbolt, making certain modifi-
cations necessitated by the change of subject.

¶ The Illustrated Introduction contains just enough
information to prepare the reader for the imaginative
enjoyment of the story.

¶ The Text (with Footnotes) is followed by HELPS
TO FURTHER STUDY, dealing with the Poet, the Eliza-
bethan Theatre, Editions of the Play, Sources and
Dates, as well as those Classic Myths referred to by the
dramatist.

¶ Then comes an APPENDIX, treating not only of the
Text of the Play, but also the acting of the drama in
school.

¶ A further section, entitled ON THINKING IT OVER,
contains suggestions for further inquiry and a number
of questions of the kind now being set in public examina-
tions. This section is divided into two parts, designed
for younger and older students respectively.

THOMAS NELSON AND SONS, LTD.

SHAKESPEARE'S
KING HENRY IV
Part I

Edited by EVELYN SMITH, B.A.

"The reader acts the play himself
in the theatre of his own mind."

---

160 pages.   Illustrated.

With Frontispiece Portrait of Henry IV

¶ The treatment of the Play is similar to that in Sir Henry Newbolt's *Richard II* (T.E.S. 31).

¶ The Introduction deals with the Historical Setting of the Drama, the Costume of the Period, and prepares the reader for the imaginative enjoyment of Shakespeare's own story.

¶ The HELPS TO FURTHER STUDY, which follows the Text, deals with (1) Shakespeare's Life and Environment to 1597; (2) The Inn and the Highway; (3) Lyly's "Euphues"; (4) Date and Sources of the Play; (5) Quarto and Folio Editions; (6) The Historical Play; (7) Stage History of the Play.

¶ A concluding section, entitled ON THINKING IT OVER, takes the form of a suggestive and searching inquiry on the characterization and workmanship of the play. The Editor makes constant reference to modern plays, and compares Shakespeare's method with that of Drinkwater and Shaw. This section is no mere collection of examination posers, but an intelligent inquiry into the mind of the poet.

¶ Interesting Exercises are given for Senior Students on variant readings of the Text.

THOMAS NELSON AND SONS, Ltd.